Encountering Naturalism
A Worldview and Its Uses

Thomas W. Clark

Center for Naturalism

ISBN 978-0-9791111-0-5

Printed in the United States of America

Published in 2007 by the Center for Naturalism

www.naturalism.org
www.centerfornaturalism.org

Contents

Acknowledgements

I'm deeply indebted to all those who took the time to comment on and correct earlier drafts of this work. Their suggestions prompted me to unclutter the style (at least a little) and clarify and extend the exposition. My particular thanks go to Ken Batts, who conceived the project and lent his encouragement and wise counsel at all stages, and to my dearest wife, whose steadfast support made this book possible.

1

Introduction & Overview

Most of us have a worldview – a set of beliefs about what exists, how reality is organized, and how we fit into it. Whether explicit or not, a worldview helps to shape our goals and actions; it's an overarching cognitive framework that helps to make sense of things, practically, ethically and existentially.

The aim of this short book is to introduce you to the science-based worldview known as naturalism. If you're interested in the big questions of human nature, human purposes and how we might best flourish here on Earth, naturalism is worth exploring.

In a nutshell, the naturalism I'll present holds that there is a single, natural, physical world in which we are completely included. There isn't a separate supernatural or immaterial realm and there's nothing supernatural or immaterial about us. Acknowledging this gives us power and self-acceptance, while keeping us compassionate, unself-righteous and open to profound experiences of meaning and connection.

Naturalism takes science, and more broadly a rational, evidence-based empiricism, as the most reliable means for discovering what exists. If we stick with science, the world is united in our understanding, not divided into the natural versus the supernatural. Science shows that each and every aspect of a human being comes from and is completely joined to the natural world, which encompasses culture as well as biology.

This naturalistic view of ourselves is of course very different from traditional religious or supernatural understandings. For example, we don't have non-physical souls that carry out our mental operations and that survive after death. Instead, the material, mortal brain is what feels, thinks and chooses. Further, scientific findings increasingly suggest that we are fully determined by our environment and genetic endowment to become who we are, and act as we do. Although we are rational agents that make real choices, we don't have free will that's independent of causality. Rather, our character, choices and behavior are traceable to factors that precede and surround us in time and space. As individuals and as social beings we are completely integrated into the unfolding of the universe in all its amazing complexity.

Because it challenges the traditional dualism of body vs. soul, and because it denies the existence of any sort of supernatural being or realm (god, devil, heaven, hell, or New Age Shangri-la), naturalism upends much Western conventional wisdom about human nature and existence. It therefore has profound implications for our personal lives, for social and planetary concerns, and for the existential questions ordinarily addressed by faith-based religions. Seeing that we're fully caused, natural beings highlights our intimate connection with the world: we are completely at home in the cosmos. It also leads to a compassionate understanding of human faults and virtues, and gives us more control over ourselves and our circumstances. The watchwords of the naturalism described here are thus *connection, compassion,* and *control.*

By understanding the causal factors that shape us and our lives – factors such as genetic endowment, upbringing and social environments – naturalism draws attention to *what works* in getting what we want. This increases individual self-efficacy and supports effective social policies in areas such as criminal and social justice, behavioral health and the environment. Further, since we understand we aren't the ultimate originators of ourselves or our behavior, we can't take ultimate credit or blame for who we are and what we do. This reduces unwarranted feelings of moral superiority, pride, shame and guilt, while encouraging self-acceptance. And since we see *others* as fully caused, for instance substance abusers, criminal offenders, the destitute and homeless, we might become less blaming, less punitive, and more empathetic and understanding. People don't create themselves, so responsibility for their character and behavior isn't ultimately theirs, but is distributed over the many factors that shaped them. Were we given their environmental and genetic lot in life, we would have become who they are and acted as they did: *there but for circumstances go I.* This challenges head-on the radical individualism of Western culture that imagines we are literally self-made. It also grounds a naturalistic ethics of compassion that guides personal behavior and motivates progressive social policy. This is an unapologetically *humanistic* naturalism.

The naturalistic worldview has roots going back to the Buddha and ancient Greeks, and a recent history that includes some of our most celebrated scientists and thinkers. It is the philosophical heart of movements such as the Enlightenment, secular humanism and freethought, and is the cognitive framework taken for granted by many scientists and philosophers. But for the most part naturalism has not been explicitly named as the comprehensive worldview that it is. Nor have its basic elements and implications been described in ordinary language for a wider audience, some of whom might find it a more plausible and effective alternative to faith-based worldviews. That said, I recommend Richard Carrier's book, *Sense and Goodness Without God*, as a comprehensive defense of naturalism for the philosophically inclined. For other recommended readings, see Appendix C.

Thus far, public awareness of naturalism has been driven mostly by debates about atheism and atheists, the faults and virtues of faith-based religion, and whether we can have meaning and morality without god (we can, I will argue). But the denial of god is just one naturalistic conclusion we reach if we take an evidence-based view of the world. A thorough-going naturalism is much more than the negative thesis of atheism, so in what follows I won't spend much time debunking deities. Others such as Julian Baggini, Daniel Dennett, Richard Dawkins and Sam Harris have explored this territory to good effect; see their books listed in Appendix C. My goal here is to explain naturalism as a positive, comprehensive worldview in which god, among other supernatural phenomena, plays no role.

This book, then, aims to advance in short compass the public understanding and appreciation of naturalism. I'll sketch the basis for naturalism, summarize its conclusions about the world and ourselves, and cover its psychological, practical, ethical, and existential consequences. The discussion in many cases is cursory, but I hope suggestive of the resources naturalism has to offer. I strongly recommend perusing Appendix A if you want further reassurances on common concerns about naturalism (it also gives considerably more detail on some issues), while Appendix B provides quotes from well known thinkers and statesmen who were skeptical about free will. For those wanting to explore naturalism further, Appendix C lists websites and further readings that go into far greater depth than is possible here. I've also put web links at the end of some chapter sections which direct you to online articles on specific topics, most of which are at Naturalism.Org.

I hope that this brief encounter with naturalism will prove useful and inspiring to you. Nature, it turns out, is enough.

2
What Do We Know?
How Do We Know It?

At the heart of naturalism is a commitment to a way of knowing about the world, a way of deciding what exists and how things fit together. This is the way of science and evidence – a rational, empirical stance about belief that requires us to question faith, tradition, authority, revelation and intuition as reliable guides to reality. A commitment to science and evidence unifies the world in our understanding and shows our complete connection to it: there's a single, natural world in which we are included. Taking an empirical stance when making claims about reality leads us to naturalism.

A Single, Natural World

First, according to naturalism, what do we fundamentally know? Well, naturalism makes a very bold claim about existence. It says that there's one natural, physical world or universe of which we are a part. There are not two different realms, the supernatural and natural. Since we are completely included in the natural world, there's nothing supernatural or non-physical about us, such as an immaterial soul. We are fully physical, material creatures, and to understand ourselves we needn't suppose we have souls, spirits or any other sort of ghostly supernatural stuff inside us. Our thoughts, experiences, feelings, decisions and behavior are all things the brain and body do.

How they do all this is, of course, a very complicated story that's still being figured out by science, but naturalism holds there's nothing non-physical involved.

That the material world, by means of biological and evolutionary processes, has produced conscious creatures that ask impertinent questions about existence is a pretty amazing fact. As the scientific story about *homo sapiens* gets filled in, it seems the "merely" physical isn't so mere after all. Atoms, molecules and chemicals, when arranged and operating properly, give rise to organisms and minds, remarkably enough. Naturalism thus *re-enchants* the physical world – we don't need the supernatural or non-physical to account for the marvels of nature, including ourselves. In fact, chalking these marvels up to something immaterial or supernatural is a bit of a cheat when compared to the intricacies of naturally evolved organic design.

Science as the Basis for Naturalism

But, you might well ask, how do you *know* there's only a single natural world instead of two worlds, the natural and the supernatural? Good question. It's important to acknowledge upfront that naturalism depends on taking rational, evidence-based empiricism, epitomized by science, as our way of knowing about what ultimately exists. This is the basic commitment naturalists make about knowledge, and it explains why they see the world as of a piece, not split into the natural vs. the supernatural.

If we commit ourselves to empirical science as our way of deciding about reality, no such split is possible because scientific explanations *unify* our view of what exists. Once something gets understood in a scientific theory the connections between it and the rest of what science understands become clear. This is what science does: it shows the pattern of connections between different things. These connections are sometimes literal physical connections, such as how our bodies are put together, and sometimes they are causal connections, such as how the wind causes a sailboat to move, or how societies develop, given human nature, climate and geography. Either way, science unifies the constituents of the known world into a single whole in which everything, whether atoms or galaxies or even *multi*verses (some hypothesize there might be many universes, of which our universe is just one), is either closely or remotely connected to everything else. This world is what we call *nature*, whatever its final dimensions and character turn out to be. Science doesn't and can't show that there's a separate supernatural world, or some sort of immaterial stuff that's categorically different from what it discovers as part of nature. So, *if* you take science and evidence-based empiricism as your way of knowing about the world, you'll be led to naturalism.

Of course, to be a scientist isn't necessarily to be a naturalist. A large minority (40%) of scientists in the US believe in god, according to a 1997 survey conducted by Edward Larson of the University of Georgia (although in a separate poll only 7% of the National Academy of Scientists, the cream of the scientific crop, counted themselves as believers). Naturalism goes *beyond* science in recommending we never resort to faith or other non-empirical ways of knowing when deciding what's real. But of course many folks, including many scientists, often resort to faith, depending on what's at stake.

The Scientific Method

Science is in the business of coming up with good explanations of what we see around us. These days we see not only with the naked eye, but with powerful new technologies that extend perception inward to the subatomic realm and outward to the vast reaches of the cosmos. In accounting for all this perceptual input, potentially shared by anyone caring to look, science has hit upon a method that gives us coherent and reliable explanations, which in turn allow us to predict and control events. Here's a thumbnail sketch of that method.

First, scientific explanations are tied closely to collective *observation and experiment*, such that claims about knowledge are made within a community of observers; truth is not a matter of personal intuition, conjecture or conventional wisdom. What's considered knowledge is therefore both empirical (based on evidence) and publicly observable or *intersubjective*, as philosophers like to put it. Second, the scientific method requires that whatever we claim to exist in the world be reasonably well specified, either in terms of directly observable characteristics or predictions coming from theories. No mysterious, unspecified forces or entities play much of a role in scientific explanations unless their hypothesized existence is very well motivated. (Example: even though it's never been directly observed, the hypothesized existence of so-called "dark matter" is motivated by robust astronomical data on galactic mass and rotation). Third, because science is specific in its claims and requires observation to back them up, its hypotheses are usually testable and thus capable of confirmation or disconfirmation.

The upshot of all this is that scientific explanations are maximally *transparent* in describing what exists and how things interact; they tend to *unify* our understanding of phenomena by showing the connections between them, even between very different scales and types; and they are *parsimonious*, in that they discount the existence of things that don't play a well-confirmed explanatory role. Moreover, evidence-based explanations are necessarily *revisable* in the light of new evidence. Scientists take pride in being able to change their minds as further data come in, for instance about the mechanisms of evolution, the reality of global warming, the neural basis for consciousness, or the dynamics of the stock market. The scientific method thus respects observed reality, not dogma, ideology or wishful thinking. As a result, it's given us extremely powerful, reliable accounts of how things work that inform most practical endeavors, whether related to health, agriculture, transportation, economics, the environment or social policy.

www.naturalism.org/science.htm#explanation

Sticking with Science

At this point you might ask: Ok, science is great stuff, but why should I stick with it in deciding what to believe about the world? Why shouldn't I use science for such things as medicine and nutrition but rely on non-empirical beliefs for other things, such as answering questions about life after death, who I really am, and my purpose here on Earth?

Well, there's no absolute reason you *must* take science as your preferred route to knowledge. But still, there are some pretty good reasons. When we need to decide something of any importance, for instance how to best treat a disease, we want the most reliable information about what works. It's science that provides the most reliable information about disease, since by and large the information it gathers is confirmed by experiment and careful observation; it isn't a matter of faith, tradition, intuition or authority, all of which can be unreliable. Science simply extends the commonsense wisdom that in order to get what we want, whether its good health or a good meal, we have to know how things work. And, (this is important!) commonsense and science say that the way things actually work, and what actually exists, are *independent* of how we might like things to be. Wishes and hopes and thoughts are one thing, the way things are is another. So if you don't want to be misled by wishful thinking or delusion, look to science and evidence, not faith or intuition.

Now, naturalists hold to science in deciding *all* the questions about what ultimately exists in the universe; they don't suddenly switch to faith or intuition when it comes to such things as the self, free will, death, consciousness, and the like. If science works well in important matters such as medicine, nutrition, energy and climate change, why suppose it suddenly stops working in these other domains? If we want factual answers to the Big Questions (to the extent that they are factual questions) why not seek the most reliable knowledge available, knowledge that's independent of wishful thinking?

Adopting a consistently empirical approach to knowledge is also *simpler* and more cognitively *satisfying*. It's simpler to use a single, evidence-based way of knowing about the world instead of switching back and forth between faith and empiricism. And scientific empiricism satisfies our desire for what we might call cognitive coherence: things fit together in science since its explanations reveal connections between phenomena, from sub-atomic particles, to plants, to planets, to galaxies.

Sometimes people turn to faith and tradition to answer particular questions since they don't like the answers offered by science. They find faith-based beliefs more reassuring, for instance the belief that the soul survives death. So here's a question about your priorities: Do you want the empirical truth backed up by evidence, or do you want to be reassured? Nothing can force you to stick with science when the going gets rough, but if you're more interested in truth than reassurance, in clear explanations more than comforting illusions, then you might be, or might become, a naturalist: someone who takes science as their guide to the whole world, including us frail, vulnerable human beings.

In denying ourselves the psychological comforts of belief in the supernatural, such as god and the soul, naturalists don't claim we can categorically *disprove* the existence of things for which there's no empirical evidence. It's notoriously difficult to prove things *don't* exist, unless they happen to be logically impossible. It's rather that we don't clutter up our model of the world by believing in them, or by reserving a possible place for them. We believe on the basis of preponderance of the evidence, and absent that, we feel we're justified in *not* believing. Similarly, naturalists can't *prove* that the scientific method is the best or only route to reliable factual knowledge about ultimate reality. It's just that no alternative method of justifying belief has emerged that rivals science in giving us a coherent, unified understanding of how things work.

Of course science doesn't pretend to have all the answers, which is one of its great virtues. But the inevitable gaps in its explanations tempt us to insert our favorite unexplained explainer, such as the soul, spirit, god or free will (see Chapter 3). To resist this temptation we must stay true to evidence, and when evidence is scarce that means remaining agnostic about what we might very much want to believe. Such is the discipline of being what we might call *cognitively responsible*.

Again, it's important to remember that the naturalist's commitment to empiricism is not itself dictated by science. To say that we shouldn't dally with faith, intuition and revelation when deciding what's real isn't a scientific claim. Rather, it's a *recommendation*, a normative stance based on good reasons (not faith!), namely, our commendable desire for reliable knowledge. It's this stance that generates naturalism as a worldview, one which discounts the existence of the supernatural. But science itself is not a worldview that holds there's nothing beyond nature; it isn't a worldview at all, only a method for justifying beliefs.

Remember also that being empirical when justifying beliefs doesn't entail *scientism*, the idea that science is the measure of all things and applies to all domains of life (see Appendix A for more on scientism). It's only to say we should base our beliefs about what exists on good, intersubjective evidence.

At first glance, the naturalist's tough-minded commitment to empirical truth might seem cold and unforgiving. But as we shall see, naturalism gives us an effective, ethically viable and emotionally satisfying understanding of reality, grounded in our most reliable way of knowing.

www.naturalism.org/science.htm

3

Who Are We?

A fundamental question most thoughtful people ask, sooner or later, is who or what are we, really? Naturalism, which insists that there's nothing supernatural about us, has a rather different answer than those offered by most traditional religions and other varieties of dualism. We don't have immaterial souls, nor is the mind separate from the body. As we've seen, naturalism holds to science in deciding the big, sometimes daunting questions about human nature, and science finds no evidence for the soul. We are what nature is doing in this particular form, what we call a person.

The Physical Person

Most basically, science shows that human beings are complicated physical organisms that evolved from simpler organisms, that in turn evolved from yet simpler organisms, such that we are historically connected to all life on the planet and thus to the planet itself. All sentient beings, including humans, owe their existence to conditions that extend far beyond them in space and time. Seeing this, we find ourselves at home in the universe, full-fledged participants in the unfolding natural order. By acknowledging our origins in evolution, the naturalist perspective can enhance our feeling of kinship with the other species and our desire to sustain and nurture our common habitat (see Chapter 6, the section on environmental concerns).

In explaining our particular organic form, science has amassed overwhelming evidence that human beings are complex, highly organized collections of atoms, molecules, cells, neurons, muscles, bone, etc., produced by natural selection. These material components, ordered in astonishingly intricate ways, are all we need to explain ourselves to ourselves. If we hold to science, there's no good reason to think that in addition we harbor immaterial souls or spirits, or any "mental" stuff inside us that's separate from our physical being.

This doesn't mean we don't have minds – the capacity to think, perceive, feel, dream, believe, plan and decide. It does mean, however, that the mind, including consciousness, is what the *brain* does, and all of this (as weird as it might seem) is somehow a fully physical process. There is no soul or spirit involved in mental activity, even though it might feel that there is. Just how the brain accomplishes all this is just beginning to be understood; we won't know the full story for many decades to come. But science is gradually making the case that the material brain does everything that the immaterial soul was supposed to do, including feel, think and choose. We don't have to be mind-body *dualists*, who suppose there are two basic categories of things in the world, mental and physical, to explain ourselves. In fact, dualism really doesn't get us very far since the interaction between soul and body is inevitably left obscure. This is why the soul doesn't survive in scientific accounts of the person: it does no explanatory work. Nevertheless, the dualistic view of ourselves strongly persists outside science, perhaps because we're to some extent biologically hard-wired to split the world conceptually into the mental and physical, as psychologist Paul Bloom suggests in his book *Descartes' Baby*. It's also comforting to suppose that something personal survives death.

Because the brain is so complex, and because each of us (except for identical twins) has a unique genetic endowment and has grown up in at least slightly different circumstances, we all end up with a unique brain that literally *embodies* our character and motives. This is the physical basis for being a distinct, identifiable human individual. So being fully physical doesn't mean we lose our individuality, one of the common concerns about naturalism (see Appendix A). All that science does is *explain*, in terms of brain development, how we get to be unique; our uniqueness doesn't disappear unless we're brainwashed to become similar in our tastes and dispositions.

Since we are fully physical, natural creatures, this means that everything we are and do is causally connected to the rest of the world, including culture and society. The scientific account of ourselves holds that we are *entirely* products of our social and family environments as they interact with our genetic endowment. The way we develop from embryos to newborns to adults is a complex process of cause and effect, described using the many different sorts of physical, chemical, biological, and behavioral regularities (or laws) that scientists have discovered. We can in principle, if not always in practice, explain our brain-based character and motives as results of that process.

Science is also describing the connections between the brain and body on the one hand and consciousness and behavior on the other. Why neural activity should be associated with subjective consciousness is of course a deep scientific and philosophical puzzle (see the books by Blackmore, Metzinger and Humphrey listed in Appendix C), and understanding the precise mechanisms by which the brain controls behavior is perhaps decades away. But should these explanations be forthcoming, with enough data we could in principle trace the genetic and environmental causes going back in time of what you're feeling, thinking and doing at this very moment. Your political opinions, for example, are traceable to genetically influenced personality traits, your upbringing in a liberal or conservative household, your education, all the campaign ads you've ever seen, and debates with friends and foe about issues of the day. All these factors left their mark on your brain and express themselves when you enter the voting booth.

www.naturalism.org/consciou.htm

Challenging Free Will

This brings us to a central (and some think disturbing) conclusion of naturalism: we don't have free will, defined as the ability to transcend causality in our choices and actions. Free will in this sense, a sense that naturalism denies, allows us to cause things to happen without ourselves being fully caused; or, if we are fully caused, we're *self*-caused in some crucial respect. We are *causally privileged* over the rest of nature. Whatever the mental and physical, internal and external conditions were at the time of a choice, we could still have chosen otherwise. We aren't completely determined in our actions, or if we are we're ultimately *self*-determined.

Now, many people suppose they have this sort of free will, but to have it you'd have to be disconnected from nature in some way, and naturalism says there's no way we're disconnected. Instead, everything we are and do derives, ultimately, from factors outside ourselves. Although there might well be irreducible randomness in nature at the micro-level of quantum mechanics, all the evidence suggests that your character and behavior are fully determined, entirely a matter of cause and effect. Why? Because they are completely dependent on the operations of your physical brain and body in which quantum indeterminism plays no explanatory role. (Of course these operations, although deterministic, aren't simple clockwork mechanisms but extremely complex processes that defy straightforward prediction.) Further, science tends to confirm the hypothesis that your brain and body are themselves fully caused phenomena that ultimately owe their existence *entirely* to the outside world, to the genetic endowment of your parents and all the environments to which you were exposed. The myriad of cause and effect relations that created you and constitute you is a continuous, unbroken causal network that extends throughout your life, and that connects you to your current environment. Your decision to read this book, for example, was one outcome of this network as it evolved right up to the moment the decision arose.

This means we *don't* have free will in the sense defined above, what philosophers sometimes call "contra-causal" free will because it goes against or transcends causality. Naturalism holds that we aren't first causes, nor are we self-caused. Self-causation is a logical impossibility: you'd first have to exist before you could cause yourself; but then, of course, you didn't cause yourself to exist. And even if it turns out that determinism – the tight, reliable, cause and effect relationship between events described in scientific laws – is false for macrolevel phenomena such as human beings, this *still* wouldn't make you the ultimate author of yourself or your actions. It would simply introduce something random and inexplicable in the process of how you came to be and how you make choices; it wouldn't give you any sort of control or self-origination. So denying determinism doesn't get you contra-causal free will, a point many tend to overlook.

It's important to note that definitions of free will vary, and that naturalism emphatically doesn't deny free will defined as choosing voluntarily to do something, of acting without being coerced. When I say I got married "of my own free will" (which I did, as it happens) that means no one was holding a gun to my head during the wedding ceremony. But I was fully and delightfully *caused* to want to get married, so this sort of free will is *compatible* with determinism. (See Daniel Dennett's books *Elbow Room* and *Freedom Evolves* for good accounts of naturalistic, "compatibilist" senses of free will, as philosophers call them.) The liberty of voluntary action I exercised in getting married is obviously of central importance to us; it's a liberty we luckily enjoy in our open society within the broad limits of law and morality. It's an uncontroversially *real* sort of freedom we all want and often have to a greater or lesser extent, depending on our circumstances. But as important as it is, we shouldn't confuse it with being free from cause and effect. (One way to avoid such confusion would be to call compatibilist freedom "free *action*," not free will.)

To say we don't have contra-causal free will is to say that we're *not* causally privileged over the rest of nature. We are not little gods who get to lord it over our neck of the woods without our character and motives, embodied in the brain, being themselves determined by our genes, upbringing and the wider culture. To think that would be to hold a supernatural view of ourselves as separate from the world in some respect, the antithesis of naturalism.

Yet another way of making this point is that from a naturalistic perspective, all our thoughts, feelings, experiences and behavior happen without there being a non-physical supervisor or soul in charge, making them happen and witnessing them. You *are* the experiences and behavior carried out by your brain and body, not something extra exerting control. There's no puppeteer inside pulling the strings, only the motivated process of being you from moment to moment, whether it's the thought arising now ("Man, this is too weird!") or the behavior arising now (turning the page, or not).

If such a puppeteer existed – an uncaused causer – we might wonder: on what basis does *it* make decisions? After all, anything uncaused or uninfluenced, riding above the flux of your motives and beliefs, would have *no reason* to choose one way or the other. So having an uncaused, uninfluenced and immaterial puppeteer in charge of your brain and body wouldn't do you any practical good.

Human Agency

Nevertheless, many think that because naturalism denies contra-causal free will, it reduces human beings to mere robots. The outraged response to behaviorist B.F. Skinner, who denied free will in his 1971 book *Beyond Freedom and Dignity*, reflected this very concern. For many, *real* freedom and dignity require that we be causal exceptions to nature. If we aren't puppeteers pulling our own strings, then human beings don't really do anything; *we* end up being the puppets – puppets of fate, robbed of our powers, of meaning, of our intrinsic worth. A few philosophers such as Saul Smilansky (see his book *Free Will and Illusion*) argue that the denial of free will is so dangerous an idea, so demoralizing – literally – that we should discourage the dissemination of naturalism. He would advise you to stop reading immediately.

But this book argues we need not fall into a moral panic about free will; we need not, and indeed should not, conceal the scientific truth about ourselves, in which case keep reading. Human persons don't disappear under naturalism, even though we can explain how they originate and develop. Without contra-causal freedom, we remain complex, autonomous creatures, who act for reasons and motives that are legitimately *ours*, not anyone else's. You don't stop being a locus of rational, effective behavior just because you were caused to be that way. Your will – expressed in your passions, plans, and actions – is just as strong as ever. And your thoughts and actions feed back into the further development of your character and motives, giving you a significant (but of course not ultimate or contra-causal) role in shaping yourself.

Some worry that to deny the existence of an inner controller means you're "out of control" in some sense. But remember, most of the time your behavior is controlled by who and what you are: a particular person, embodied by a physical organism that's been taught to behave in mostly socially acceptable ways (I trust!). It turns out the brain is a very reliable, robust repository of the moral rules that for the most part keep behavior within acceptable limits. So you don't run amok without the supervisory soul (but please, protect your brain when biking and rollerblading). Our physically-based abilities to feel, think, and decide are essential and ineliminable parts of the causal story behind ethical action: they "add value" that can be added in no other way. So we don't cease being real moral agents who make real, controlled choices.

Nor does naturalism mean you lose your own *causal powers* to influence things and make things happen. If you discover in yourself a burning desire to save the whales, or all the other species now in danger of extinction, you can join Greenpeace and likely make a difference. All that's changed is that you understand clearly where your desires and your powers come from; they aren't ultimately self-caused. In fact, to really understand yourself *requires* understanding the deterministic, cause and effect relationships between the events of your life. This always shows your motives and actions to be fully a function of prior circumstances, plus your current situation. As we'll see in Chapter 5, such knowledge might well add to your power and self-control.

Now, it may *seem* as if we are uncaused or self-caused in some respect; after all, we can't peer into our own brains and see the various processes and causes at work. It just feels as if this interior mental self thinks and acts and decides from moment to moment without any causal antecedent, without anything determining what it does. Further, the sense of being a self *seems* quintessentially mental or immaterial, in that I can't pin down its physical correlate. But neuroscience is on the way to showing how causation works in the brain, how the feeling of being an uncaused, immaterial self might be an emergent property of what your brain does as it models your body interacting with the world. Thomas Metzinger suggests in *Being No One* that such a feeling might be an adaptive trait for a complex creature to have, even if we don't literally have such a self. So: don't take your intuition of being a freely willing mental agent or soul as a necessarily accurate reflection of reality. For a fascinating account of the unconscious mechanics of the sense of agency, try Daniel Wegner's *The Illusion of Conscious Will.*

If you have to choose between your gut intuitions about who you fundamentally are and science (and you might well have to), I recommend sticking with science, however uncomfortable this might seem at first. In later chapters and in Appendix A, I hope to relieve any, or at least most, discomfort you might have with what naturalism says about the self and its choices. And besides, as Chet Raymo points out in *Skeptics and True Believers*, the naturalistic conception of self doesn't lessen us, quite the opposite:

> To admit that the mind is electrochemical does not diminish our concept of self; rather, it suggests that the cosmos was charged with the possibility of becoming conscious from the first moment of creation. The newly emerging concept of self is materialistic and mechanistic; it is also capacious enough to embrace not only the future but also the past, and expansive enough to entangle the self with the rest of creation.

The entangled, natural self is what the denial of supernatural free will reveals: not a passive puppet, but the concrete, actualized personal process that nature accomplishes in all its human manifestations.

Regarding free will, in Appendix B you'll find quotes from well known philosophers, scientists and even statesmen who were skeptical about contra-causal freedom. The consensus among most philosophers these days is that such freedom is conceptually incoherent and therefore, as Daniel Dennett puts it, not worth wanting. Likewise, most biologists, neuroscientists, cognitive scientists and psychologists think that contra-causal free will is empirically unmotivated: it doesn't do any explanatory *work* in scientific accounts of consciousness or behavior. So if you end up a free will skeptic yourself, you'll be in good company. For more on living without the myth of contra-causal freedom, see the link below, the books recommended at the end of Chapter 5, and the publications of Susan Blackmore, Joshua Greene, Heidi Ravven and Tamler Sommers at their home pages on the Web.

A final advisory about naturalism and determinism: they are by no means and in no sense equivalent. Naturalism is a worldview that accepts what science says about ourselves. Determinism is the idea that reliable cause and effect relations exist between events, such that specific causes reliably produce specific effects. If determinism should prove false in any instance, that doesn't imply the existence of a supernatural realm, nor, as we've seen above, would it give us contra-causal free will. A naturalistic view of ourselves incorporates determinism *and* indeterminism, in whatever measure they apply to the natural world.

www.naturalism.org/freewill.htm

4
Nothing New:
A Brief History of Naturalism

Before discussing the implications and consequences of naturalism, I first want to show that it's been with us for quite some time, although it hasn't until relatively recently been named as such. To count yourself a naturalist will make you heir to a long and distinguished tradition of thought, even if thus far naturalists have constituted a small minority in a world largely committed to supernaturalism and mind-body dualism. (Note: except for the section on the Buddha, this chapter is based largely on Ignacio Prado's essay "Ionian Enchantment: A Brief History of Scientific Naturalism," for which I'm most grateful. It can be found at the link directly below.)

www.naturalism.org/history.htm

The Greeks

There's no definitive consensus about who were the first naturalists, but several of the ancient Greeks are candidates for this honor. In particular, we know that the 7th century BCE Greek philosopher Thales thought that all existence was a single substance that takes multiple forms. Such *ontological monism* (as opposed to dualism) holds there's nothing irreducibly mental, volitional or personal in nature. Instead, the mind, will and person are composite phenomena, all created out of insensate matter. This bold claim (only now being fleshed out by neuroscience) was matched by the equally revolutionary idea, advocated by the Greek sophist Protagoras, that knowledge is best grounded in systematic observation and rational inquiry, not in tradition, priestly authority, omens or oracles. Such *rational empiricism* is of course the basis of the modern scientific method, and was also found in the work of the Greek philosopher Democritus, who advocated a materialist view of nature composed of indivisible atoms and the void.

The Greeks were not only students of nature but of human relations. Philosophers such as Socrates, Epicurus, Aristotle, and the Stoics sought to construct systems of ethics that were essentially naturalistic insofar as they didn't appeal to divine authority. Justice and morality could, they argued, be grounded in principles flowing from the rational pursuit of individual and social flourishing. Here, perhaps, was first articulated the naturalistic claim that we can be good without god.

The Buddha

In a very different part of the world (India), and coming out of a very different philosophical tradition (Vedanta), the Buddha hit upon a naturalistic conception of existence and the self. There are no indestructible material or spiritual essences, he said; instead, reality is an ever-changing flux in which all phenomena are impermanent and arise interdependently. The personal self is not the unchanging soul-essence it appears to be, but an ephemeral construction of impersonal factors. Just as early Greek naturalists challenged the existence of supernatural deities, the Buddha challenged the Vedic postulate of a permanent soul or *atman.*

Although his was an *introspective* empiricism focused on human experience, not publicly observable events, the Buddha's conclusions have a distinctly modern cast. Some modern day physical theories challenge the idea of any essential indivisible "stuff" in nature, while neuroscientific explanations of the sense of self suggest it's a moment-to-moment construction of brain processes, not an abiding essence. The Buddha's claims about existence and the self were incorporated into a very practical and naturalistic ethics: compassion, for ourselves and others, is gained by seeing the truth of our impermanence and interdependence; no supernatural moral imperative is necessary. All told, between the Greeks and the Buddha it seems the basis for scientific naturalism, along with some of its major implications, was in place well before the modern era.

The Enlightenment and Renaissance

From these ancient roots, rediscovered in the Renaissance and developed during the Enlightenment, sprang the cumulative, empirically grounded and explicitly rational mode of understanding we call science. The history of early scientists and Renaissance luminaries such as Copernicus, Kepler, Galileo, and Leonardo Da Vinci largely concerns the discovery of a method of inquiry that would produce a reliable, predictive model of reality. This *empirical* method contradicted the long-held assumption that claims about the fundamental nature of existence are the province of religious authority. As a result, proponents of the new science found themselves in opposition to the Church, both in their conclusions about the world and in how these were reached.

In the mid 17th century, Dutch philosopher Baruch Spinoza developed an explicitly monistic view of reality in which he identified god with impersonal nature, in effect uniting the supernatural and natural realms. This denial of dualism won him excommunication from his Jewish religious community. Nevertheless, with the help of the irrepressible French Enlightenment *philosophes* such as Voltaire, Diderot and Condorcet, Spinoza's impolitic questioning of dogma became a celebrated intellectual virtue. Inquiry in both science and philosophy gradually freed itself from the limits of religion, and so was born the possibility of an explicitly naturalistic view of the world. British philosophers such as Hobbes and Hume, and later Bentham and Mill, developed naturalistic approaches to logic, political theory, epistemology and metaphysics, making appeals to god and religious authority unnecessary.

Of course there was, and remains, considerable resistance to the rise of secular science and philosophy – the basis for naturalism – simply because it calls traditional faith-based accounts of reality into question. The most virulent opposition to the naturalistic revolution was of course generated by Charles Darwin, whose theory of evolution holds that natural selection, not intelligent design, explains the form and function of all living creatures, including ourselves. Thomas Henry Huxley ("Darwin's bulldog") articulated what was at stake in his 1892 essay "Naturalism and Supernaturalism," a trenchant historical analysis of conflicting worldviews; see the link immediately below.

http://www.gutenberg.org/files/16474/16474-h/16474-h.htm

The Modern Era

Naturalism, named as such, first surfaced in American philosophical thought early in the 20th century. The American Naturalists, as they were sometimes called, included John Dewey, George Santayana, Fredrick Woodbridge and John Randall. They conceived of philosophy as more or less continuous with science, not its foundation, and they sought an explicitly monistic, as opposed to dualistic, understanding of mind, ethics and ultimate reality. Taking the empirical science of Bacon, Newton, Maxwell and Einstein as the touchstone of reliable knowledge, they saw no explanatory need or justification to posit a *super*natural realm, hence the name "naturalists." The current Western philosophical mainstream, growing out of the work of mid-twentieth century naturalist philosophers such as W.V.O. Quine and Wilfred Sellars, largely accepts scientific naturalism as its governing cognitive framework, although vigorous academic debate continues about its basis and limits. Some Christian philosophers and theologians, notably Alvin Plantinga (*Naturalism Defeated?*) and John F. Haught (*Is Nature Enough?*), argue that naturalism can't ground or explain human rationality and ethics, although they don't offer a clear account of how a supernatural divinity does better. (Of course any such account would tend to *naturalize* god by showing how he, she or it interacts with the material world humans inhabit.)

Although naturalism will always be subject to debate – see for instance De Caro and Macarthur's *Naturalism in Question* – it's now the default working assumption for a majority of academics and scientists, at least in their professional dealings with questions of fact. Outside divinity schools and churches, appeals to religious authority, sacred texts and faith-based tradition play almost no role in modern accounts of how the world works and how human beings and societies function. Rather, science and empiricism rule as the largely unchallenged arbiters of what constitutes reliable knowledge about human nature and the cosmos. We find ourselves with a mature, rationally well-grounded way of knowing that, when taken as definitive, points to a fully natural universe.

Still, taken not just as a cognitive framework or method but as a comprehensive *worldview*, naturalism is nearly unheard of nowadays except among relatively small groups of humanists, skeptics and atheists (see for instance the websites of the American Humanist Association, the Council for Secular Humanism and the Skeptic Society listed in Appendix C). As emphasized in Chapter 2, a fully developed naturalistic worldview goes beyond science since it holds (for good reasons) that we should rely solely on rational empiricism in deciding what ultimately exists. If we do, we achieve a satisfying, unified picture of ourselves as physical beings completely at home in the natural world. Seeing how naturalism applies to personal, social, and existential concerns, as set forth in the following chapters, will help realize its potential as a practical and inspiring worldview.

5
The Self and Relationships

Having surveyed the basics of naturalism, and knowing something of its history, we're now in a position to consider its implications. How might the view of ourselves as natural creatures, fully connected to the world and caused by circumstances outside us, affect our beliefs, attitudes and behavior? We'll work from the inside out, starting with the self. Then we'll look at our relationships with others, see how naturalism might influence our thinking on social policy, and finally take up the big-picture questions of meaning and purpose in a natural universe.

Connection, Self-Acceptance and Self-Efficacy

There are several important personal implications of naturalism that make it a useful and inspiring worldview. First, by seeing that you are indeed completely caused to be who you are, both physically and psychologically, you discover yourself fully connected to the material and social world around you, and ultimately to the cosmos that generated our galaxy, solar system and planet. You discover yourself, a person, to be completely *at home* in what looks to be, finally, an impersonal, non-purposive universe. This is the basis for what we might call a naturalistic spirituality, an approach to existential questions that celebrates the strange and wonderful fact that nature transcends the demand for ultimate meaning. We'll explore this in Chapter 7.

Second, naturalism shows that since you didn't create yourself,

you can't take ultimate credit for who you are in the way traditional supernatural notions of the self make possible; only supernatural
souls have contra-causal free will that endows them with ultimate
credit. You, a natural creature, have to share credit for your successes
and good deeds with all those conditions – people, places, things,
and genes – that made you a good person. Even your striving for
goodness has its causal roots, perhaps in parental expectations and an
inherited predilection for empathy and selfless action. When we see
the causal story behind virtue, there are no longer grounds for feeling
morally superior, prideful, self-important, arrogant, or for holding
any other self-aggrandizing attitude or belief about yourself. Just be
grateful for your good fortune.

Third, and for the same reasons, you can't take ultimate *blame*
for being nasty, selfish, lazy, fearful, or any other personal failing.
These characteristics too are fully caused, owing their existence to
a host of genetic and environmental conditions: your parents (their
genes *and* parenting skills), your community, peer group, schools,
and all the unpredictable happenstances of your life. Seeing that you
don't have contra-causal freedom reduces unnecessary and counter-
productive guilt and shame aimed at the self for its sins. Remember
though, the fact that being nasty and selfish is fully caused doesn't
mean you shouldn't stop being nasty and selfish. We don't lose our
moral compass in accepting naturalism (more on this later).

Fourth, when we understand we are not self-made and can't take
ultimate credit or blame, we might discover a deep, abiding acceptance of ourselves and our situation. There's no causally privileged
agent who could have done otherwise in the circumstances of your
life as it unfolded; all your decisions, good and bad, arose without
benefit of a supernatural self that made things happen as they did.
This rather startling realization, so contrary to the Western assumption that individuals can (and should) transcend their circumstances,

releases us from the regret, protest, shame and guilt wrapped up in the supposition that we could have done otherwise as a situation developed. Seeing that, for instance, I was fully determined to do badly in a job interview prevents me from wasting hours or days in self-recrimination, time I could spend more productively in preparing for the next one.

On a larger scale, appreciating the full scope of the causal network that is nature – a process that far, far transcends us – grounds a stable acceptance of *what is* in all its manifestations, personal and global. Such acceptance, although it might seem like passive resignation from the standpoint of Western radical individualism, actually works as a sturdy foundation upon which to pursue our projects, less vulnerable to the slings and arrows of our own reactive psychology. This isn't to deny the importance of our strivings, but to put them in a wider perspective that might give us some measure of serenity. Although achieving serenity is rarely mentioned as a goal in our hyper-competitive culture, it's arguably central to mental health, in which case naturalistic acceptance works greatly to our personal advantage. (For further discussion of agency and individualism see Appendix A, and for more on acceptance and serenity see Paul Breer's *The Spontaneous Self*, the chapter on "Psychological Implications of Giving Up Free Will.")

Fifth, and lastly, here's what naturalism gives you in a practical sense, although as you may have noticed the "you" has changed quite a bit. By understanding that you are caused, and by seeing just *how* you are caused, you gain *control and power* over yourself. Instead of supposing you can just will yourself to be other than you are (stronger, smarter, more altruistic), you understand that self-change and effective action flow from concrete conditions. Create the right conditions, then self-change and self-efficacy will follow. Want to be more productive or creative? Investigate the factors that permit productivity and creativity, then go about creating them. Choreographer Twyla Tharp gives us a nice example of this process in her book *The Creative Habit*, and B. F. Skinner suggests techniques for effective self-management in *About Behaviorism*. Even the desire to change has its antecedents in conditions, so if you want to want to change, you can arrange for that as well.

Of course it isn't always easy to discover what the right conditions are for self-transformation, or to actually create them, but it's a better bet than supposing that the motivation and ability to change will arise independently of such conditions. Moreover, there has to be at least an inkling of desire (or desire to desire) to begin with, otherwise the process can't get started. If such an inkling arises, then knowing how to nourish it is an essential step in self-transformation, and that requires knowledge of cause and effect, not reliance on willpower. By challenging the idea that you have a freely willing soul that can just *choose* to change, you discover your real source of power: understanding your causality through and through. Remember though, it's likely you'll encounter problems you can't solve on your own, however much you learn about yourself and your situation. In which case the wise course is to get the help you need. After all, as the Buddha taught, we are interdependent by nature.

www.psychologicalselfhelp.org/Chapter14/chap14_54.html

Relationships, Compassion and Healing

The implications of naturalism that apply to yourself apply to others, and for the same reasons. Knowing that people are fully caused to be as they are, and couldn't have done otherwise in the circumstances they were in, you're going to be much less likely to assign them ultimate credit and blame. This means you're less likely to cling to feelings such as resentment, anger and contempt. As Spinoza said long ago about determinism: "This doctrine teaches us to hate no one, to despise no one, to mock no one, to be angry with no one, and to envy no one." The person at the office who drives you crazy with his arrogance is completely a function of his formative and current conditions (including you!), which should give you pause before indulging in revenge fantasies. Of course, we're all prone to such responses since we evolved to have the capacity for anger and resentment for good reasons: to get those who treat us poorly to shape up. But once we see clearly that those who mistreat us aren't self-made, it's easier to let such feelings go once they stop playing a useful role.

Those who act badly are not the *ultimate* source of their misdeeds, only the proximate source. To concentrate blame solely on them ignores the historical factors that shaped them as individuals and the current conditions that now determine their behavior. Further, had you been in their genetic and environmental shoes, you'd be acting identically. This doesn't alter the judgment that they should mend their ways, but it might attenuate feelings of anger or moral superiority. It also makes it easier to forgive, when forgiveness is warranted.

Understanding that people aren't self-made can help heal troubled relationships, since you won't hold grudges for as long, or waste so much time resenting someone or plotting to get even. Petty arguments will remain just that, petty, without getting out of control. You'll be able to grin and bear someone's foibles, maybe even give them useful feedback instead of shunning or swearing at them. You won't, of course, become a saint (nobody likes a saint anyway), but you might become more compassionate and forgiving if you appreciate the fact that they, like yourself, are the natural unfolding of a complex set of causal processes, those that constitute a human being. They are not first causes that are simply *choosing* to be nasty, lazy, arrogant or self-centered.

All of psychology and sociology, to the extent they are scientific disciplines, operate on the premise that human beings and their behavior result from specific conditions, not contra-causal free will. So if you discount the existence of the freely willing soul you're simply aligning yourself with our best practical, evidence-based self-knowledge. Although some might think so, this is not to take a dehumanizing view of ourselves; science doesn't deny anyone's humanity or worth. People remain people – inescapably precious to us – despite the fact that they are entirely natural phenomena. Parental and marital affection, admiration for talent and achievement, appreciation for self-sacrifice and courage – all these survive without supposing that persons choose their virtues without being caused to do so. We are inescapably gripped by our basic, hard-wired dispositions to love and seek love, and to value those personal qualities that most contribute to human flourishing.

It's also important to see that taking the naturalistic perspective on others does *not* mean you become non-judgmental or passive in the face of abuse, or stop looking out for yourself. Standards of right and wrong still apply and it's important to enforce them unequivocally. But naturalism – the unwavering understanding and acceptance of causality – makes it difficult to justify reveling in punishment or revenge; we only do what's necessary to protect ourselves and prevent future wrong-doing. This insight of course relates to criminal justice policy; see below in Chapter 6.

Finally, and significantly from a practical standpoint, naturalism permits us to be wiser in setting up conditions under which we behave well toward each other. After all, since actions always result from causes, not from free will, we can learn to control those causes to our benefit and the benefit of others we interact with. If you have a relationship that's troubled, look at the whole situation carefully, yourself included, instead of simply pointing the finger at your partner, child, co-worker or friend. If someone's behaving badly, there's a reason, a cause, a set of conditions that's contributing to the behavior, and these have to be addressed.

Again, this doesn't mean that anger and discipline are never appropriate, but it does mean they should be applied judiciously and compassionately. When you find yourself asking, irritably and rhetorically, "Why the hell does he keep doing that?!", I strongly recommend you *answer the rhetorical question*. The causal story revealed in the answer, which always has roots outside the person, might reduce counter-productive blaming and contempt, *and* it will give you vital information about how the behavior might be changed. Such psychological and practical insights can help heal relationships that might otherwise fall apart, should we cling to a supernatural understanding of human nature.

Responsibility without Free Will

When interacting with others, we inevitably have expectations about what's good behavior and, more momentously, about what's right and wrong. To behave ethically and responsibly we have to have standards and enforce them. But there's a question that often arises when people consider the implications of naturalism: on what grounds can we hold people responsible if their actions are fully determined? There are a few steps in the explanation.

First, even if we don't have supernatural free will independent of determining causes, it remains true that we very much want certain things to happen and very much *don't* want other things to happen. We very much want to live, and don't want to die. We love our friends and families (maybe even some of our neighbors) and we want them and our communities kept safe and secure. As mentioned earlier, we are inescapably *gripped* by our values, precisely because they constitute us (along with other dispositions and characteristics) as organic, natural creatures. This means that even without contra-causal freedom we are strongly motivated to want certain outcomes in life, namely for ourselves and our loved ones to flourish. In turn, this means we still want people, including ourselves, to act in ways to ensure this flourishing, which generally means behaving morally: not stealing, cheating, lying, or murdering. So we don't lose our values or moral norms in accepting naturalism.

Now, since people are fully caused creatures, this means they can be *caused* to behave morally. And one of the main ways we cause them to behave morally is by holding them responsible and accountable. You say to them, "If you act deliberately to endanger my child, then we will take steps to lock you up. If you try to hurt my child, I will hold you responsible, so you better not." People that we warn in this fashion, those capable of having their behavior shaped by the prospect of being held accountable, are *moral agents*. That includes just about every sane, mentally competent person over the age of 16 or so, although some kids grow up sooner than others. This means we don't need to be self-caused or have contra-causal free will to be held responsible or to be moral agents. In fact, all this would be impossible if people actually had the supernatural power to act independently of causes, since they could just ignore the prospect of being held responsible and do whatever they darn well pleased.

It's important to see that a human exemption from determinism, unlikely but not impossible, wouldn't help to make us morally responsible agents. Imagine some random, indeterministic element that affected your behavior. Suppose, bizarrely enough, that a cosmic ray triggered a neural spike that caused you to yell "Praise the lord!" at an atheist convention. Could you reasonably be blamed for that? Obviously not. Indeterminism makes the connection between your motives and your actions *less*, not more, reliable, robbing you of legitimate responsibility. As philosopher David Hume pointed out over 250 years ago, to be responsible is for our character and motives to reliably determine our behavior, so determinism is a *necessary condition* of (non-ultimate) responsibility. If, as seems the case, our character and motives are themselves fully determined by factors that ultimately we had no control over – our genetics, upbringing, peer group, etc. – they are nevertheless the main proximate causes of our behavior. Since the self is nothing over and above character and motives (it isn't an immaterial supervisor sitting somewhere in the head, as we saw in Chapter 3), we can properly say "*I* control my actions, not anyone else," at least in cases when no one's compelling us to act against our will. So human agents as the (non-ultimate) authors of behavior don't disappear on a naturalistic understanding of ourselves.

For further reassurances about responsibility and agency please see Appendix A. For more on naturalistic approaches to free will, ethics and moral responsibility, I recommend the books listed in Appendix C by William Casebeer, Patricia Churchland, Daniel Dennett, Richard Double, Gary Drescher, Owen Flanagan, Ted Honderich, Derk Pereboom, Steven Pinker, Bruce Waller, and Daniel Wegner.

www.naturalism.org/lexicon.htm

6

Naturalism and Progressive Policy

When considering the implications of naturalism for social policy, the same attitudes that naturalism inspires about yourself and your immediate community extend outward to strangers and society at large. To adopt a naturalistic view of ourselves – to see our full causal connection to the physical and social world – can influence our thinking in domains such as criminal and social justice, behavioral health, the environment, education and international conflict. Appreciating that persons are not self-made, but completely a function of environmental and genetic circumstances, lends support to humanistic, progressive and effective policies.

Criminal Justice

The criminal justice system in the US is shaped by beliefs about retributive punishment that motivate extremely punitive sanctions, among them the death penalty and harsh, non-rehabilitative prison conditions. Support for retribution stems at least partially from a supernaturalist conception of the criminal, who, it is commonly thought, could have chosen *not* to commit the crime whatever his internal and external circumstances might have been. Thus offenders deeply deserve punishment because they could have overcome these circumstances and acted otherwise, but simply and willfully refused to do so. This sense of strong, ultimate responsibility is used to justify inflicting suffering on offenders far beyond what's necessary for deterrence or public safety. Such retribution simply models and perpetuates retaliatory behavior, leaving in its wake vast, unnecessary trauma and degradation.

To the extent that criminality is thought to arise from individuals' self-caused, freely willed choices, its actual biological, social and economic causes will necessarily go unexplored and unaddressed. The myth of contra-causal free will essentially lets us off the hook; it releases us from our responsibility to thoroughly investigate and remedy the origins of anti-social behavior, which lie in mental illness, poverty, child abuse, and lack of education and economic opportunity. Free will is the bottom line excuse and justification for laissez-faire social policies which, by denying causation, guarantee continuing high levels of dysfunction and alienation, and which therefore perpetuate the cycle of crime and punishment. The emphasis on retribution, often based in the myth of the supernatural soul, is thus *ineffective* as well as unethically punitive. See Joshua Greene and Jonathan Cohen's paper, "For the law, neuroscience changes nothing and everything" for a critique of retribution along these lines (linked at the web page listed below).

When we come to appreciate the causal story behind crime, we won't any longer suppose that offenders create themselves and thus deserve to be punished whether or not it brings about any good consequences. Moreover, we'll pay far more attention to criminogenic factors; we'll seek to *prevent* crime instead of merely punishing it after the fact. True, it is individuals who commit offenses. They must be dealt with, compassionately and effectively. But the reasons they become offenders in the first place lie in the conditions that created them, so we must hold *society* responsible – ourselves, our families, schools, and communities, as well as offenders – in our quest for a safe, flourishing culture. A major contribution of applied naturalism will be enlightened reform of our criminal justice system: to make its main mission crime prevention, not the infliction of punishment for punishment's sake.

www.naturalism.org/criminal.htm

Social Justice

Rooted in Western culture is the widespread assumption of radical individualism, the supposition that persons are at bottom self-made. This works to justify and excuse the increasing disparities in material well-being and social advantages that have followed the dismantling of the 1960's "Great Society." On the supernaturalist, soul-based understanding of ourselves, those that fail economically fail partially because of a freely-willed refusal to apply themselves or follow the rules. Since it was their self-caused *choice* not to get ahead, some think they deserve their impoverishment. Likewise, those that succeed deserve their riches, however excessive or disproportionate, since they made themselves who they are. The huge and growing inequalities between rich and poor, exacerbated by conservative policies such as tax cuts for the wealthy and disinvestments in public infrastructure and education, are tolerated partially because they are thought by many to reflect differences in merit derived from the exercise of free will. Inequality, at bottom, is simply the reflection of what people deserve.

To the extent that economic and social inequalities are believed to result from human choices unaffected by surrounding conditions (the definition of contra-causal free will), such inequalities will be perceived as the natural outcome of self-originated individual differences, not anything that could or should be remedied by social policy. Interventions to reduce inequality will only be thought capable of operating around the margins of what is essentially up to self-caused human choices. The free will assumption thus disempowers and defeats policies to reduce inequality in advance by implying they cannot be effective, or that they somehow infringe our right to ultimate self-determination. (Of course if we really had contra-causal free will, our self-determination couldn't be infringed upon.)

In challenging the myth of radical individualism, science-based naturalism shows that a person's economic and social success is *entirely* a function of family status at birth, innate talents, access to education and other social resources, and numerous other environmental and biological factors. We can't take credit for what's ultimately a matter of lucky genes and lucky social status at birth. There are no literally self-made men or women that deeply deserve their fortunes. In defending the estate tax, Bill Gates Sr. and Chuck Collins at United for a Fair Economy point out that we don't make it on our own in becoming successful (see the UFE website listed in Appendix C). Even the disposition to work hard, compete and get ahead is entirely a matter of causal factors: good parental role models, a teacher's high expectations for achievement, perhaps even a genetically influenced capacity for industriousness. All this is the luck of the draw. Philosopher John Rawls writes in *A Theory of Justice*: "It seems to be one of the fixed points of our considered judgments that no one deserves his place in the distribution of native endowments, any more than one deserves one's initial starting place in society. The assertion that a man deserves the superior character that enables him to make the effort to cultivate his abilities is equally problematic; for his character depends in large part upon fortunate family and social circumstances for which he can claim no credit."

Accepting a naturalist view of ourselves will therefore weaken justifications for inequality based on the notion of deserved success or failure. Those of us living comfortable lives will see that *but for circumstances* we, just like the homeless camped out under the highway, would have been denied our comforts. This insight might increase our empathetic identification with the plight of the less fortunate. It will also help undercut support for social policies, such as tax breaks for the rich, that have generated huge discrepancies in wealth and opportunity, while increasing support for interventions that improve both opportunities and outcomes for the disadvantaged. Although incentives must still exist to encourage hard work, initiative and risk-taking, they need not and should not result in a grossly skewed distribution of resources. A naturalism that accepts causality will help shift the justification for having a reasonable standard of living from getting what you *deserve*, on the basis of self-caused merit, to getting what you *need* to live a fulfilled, satisfying life.

www.naturalism.org/social_justice.htm

Behavioral Health

From a naturalistic standpoint, behavioral disorders such as addiction, obesity and mental illness are understood to be determined by the complex interaction of a person's genetics and environment. For example, certain variants of genes regulating the production of dopamine in the brain can create a predisposition for addiction, which when combined with the availability of drugs (nicotine, alcohol, and illegal substances) or gambling, can produce dependence. Seeing the causal story behind an addict helps to undercut the moral stigma associated with failures of will. After all, you too would have suffered the same fate had you been dealt his genetic and environmental hand. You, like the addict, don't have a supernatural power of choice that could have overcome those conditions; you were simply lucky and he was not.

Further (and this point should sound familiar by now) understanding the causes of behavioral health problems – what we used to

consider freely-willed choices – increases tremendously our ability
to prevent and cure them. Knowing that those ensnared by chronic
depression are suffering from a brain-based illness, not a self-chosen
character flaw, is the first crucial step in getting treatment. While
some behavioral problems, such as obesity, are partially the result of
a person's voluntary behavior, we now understand that voluntary behavior too is fully determined by a person's biological and environmental situation. To the extent we understand precisely *why* someone
chooses to overeat, or drink, or smoke, we gain leverage over the
problem. The naturalistic causal model that shows how behavior arises from circumstances generates compassion *and* gives us control.

www.naturalism.org/addictio.htm

The Progressive Implications of Naturalism

The policy issues considered thus far suggest there's a link between
being a naturalist and being progressive. Once we admit that people
aren't self-made, that there but for circumstances go I, we likely become more empathetic and compassionate, attributes widely con-
ceded to be more typical of liberals than conservatives. (This is why
"compassionate conservatism" seems such a transparent attempt at
rebranding.) Furthermore, we pay greater attention to the wider, sys-
temic causes and conditions that shape individuals, again a mark of
progressive thinking. We don't blame the victim and simply call for
more "personal responsibility," a typically conservative-libertarian
solution to social problems. Finally, the naturalist's commitment to
evidence makes her more likely to challenge social and economic inequalities based on non-empirical claims about the world, for instance
the subordinate status of women, infidels and homosexuals historically endorsed by Christianity and Islam, or the financial advantages
to corporations gained by downplaying scientific findings on pollu-

tion and global warming. Progressives, not conservatives, are known for pressing such challenges. For insightful discussion of liberal and conservative worldviews and how these get expressed in policy, I recommend George Lakoff's *Moral Politics*. For more on the progressive implications of naturalism, see the links directly below.

www.naturalism.org/politics.htm#humanists
www.naturalism.org/progressivepolitics.htm

Environmental Policy

Because naturalism shows our deep connection to the world and others, it helps to prompt concern for the natural environment and for those who will succeed us on the planet. Since it discounts the existence of the soul and survival after death, naturalism increases the importance we attach to this, our only life, and the world we inhabit *now*. By acknowledging our origins in evolution, the naturalist perspective can also enhance our feeling of kinship with other species. All living creatures, not just us, owe their existence to conditions that must be sustained if they are to survive and flourish. Such considerations can help spur us to action on behalf of the planet.

To save the Earth from environmental degradation and preserve biodiversity, it's essential to take a naturalistic causal perspective, both on the factors that promote sustainability and that affect human motivation. As Jared Diamond shows in his ground-breaking book *Collapse*, earlier human societies succumbed to environmental failure brought about by heedless over-exploitation of resources such as forests and wildlife. Knowing the deterministic story behind cultures that in hindsight were doomed is absolutely necessary if we are to be properly cognizant of the hazards ahead. Practical wisdom only derives from accepting the full scope of causality, including the causes of a society's long-term success or failure. Otherwise it's likely that history will repeat itself, this time on a planetary scale.

If we want to avoid global environmental collapse, we must also create the *political will* to make sustainability a first priority. This in turn requires understanding the determinants of human motivation – we can't suppose that we will *just choose* to become committed environmentalists. Our collective desire for sustainability is itself a function of specific causes, and it's unlikely it will manifest itself in sufficient measure without deliberate motivational engineering on our part (for ideas on how to generate the political will for sustainability, see "Avoiding Collapse: Determinism, Altruism and the Creation of Political Will" linked at the end of this section). Freeing ourselves from the myth of radical, supernatural freedom is an important factor in developing the collective commitment to save the planet. Understanding our determinants, applied to global self-control, is perhaps one of the more momentous contributions a full-fledged naturalism can make toward human flourishing.

As in other applications of naturalism, *understanding the causal story* is essential – in this case, to become wise stewards of the environment. Seeing ourselves as integral parts of the natural order, not causally privileged over it, is key both for motivating concern and for developing effective policies for sustainability. See Edward O. Wilson's *The Future of Life* and *The Creation*, among his many other works, for an inspiring call to action. Al Gore's *An Inconvenient Truth* is of course required reading, or watching.

www.naturalism.org/environment.htm

Political Discourse and International Conflict

Naturalism produces the fundamental insight that our opponents and enemies, whether political, ethnic, religious or otherwise, are *not* self-created monsters. However misguided we suppose them to be, we can't suppose that given their circumstances they could have believed and acted other than they did. Conservatives, for instance, have certain personality traits and cognitive predispositions that lead them to support particular policies. These traits and predispositions are fully determined, partially by genetic endowment and partially by upbringing, peer groups and education. If you find conservative policies on poverty, criminal justice, human rights and affirmative action lamentable, remember that conservatives haven't willfully chosen to be that way; they're *caused* to be that way, so don't set them up as the devil. And likewise for bleeding heart liberals. There's a causal story to be told about their weaknesses and blind spots as well, poor things. The upshot is that in light of naturalism our political discourse might become less confrontational and contemptuous. Seeing that all of us, including our opponents, arise completely out of circumstances, we might become less susceptible to the moral outrage and demonization that's polarized political debate in the US.

The same lesson applies in the international arena. If, for instance, the Israelis and Palestinians understood each other not as self-created evil-doers who willfully disobey Allah's or Yahweh's commandments, but as products of deterministic social and geo-political processes, this might reduce the mutual hatred that drives conflict in the Middle East. Territorial disputes will still remain, of course, but the possibilities for resolution might increase once both sides see that their opposing agendas are *completely* a function of contingent circumstances. My enemy is who *I* would have been, but for an accident of birth and culture, so can I continue to regard him as evil incarnate? If not, perhaps we can talk.

The idea that we are little gods, that at bottom we just *choose* ourselves in some respect independently of genetic and environmental circumstances, arguably helps to motivate ethnic conflict and genocide. After all, that's what allows us to deeply blame and resent the "other": they could have risen above their circumstances and been good people like us if they'd only *chosen* to, using their contra-causal free will. Unlimited retaliation and revenge find justification in the idea that our enemies are not ultimately subject to causes, but are instead self-created in some crucial respect. All blame attaches to them as individuals and little or none to the conditions that created them, including our very own actions, a perfect prescription for inciting hatred.

On the other hand, once we appreciate that our ideological, ethnic and religious antagonists are fully determined to believe and act the way they do, we cannot continue to demonize them. They, like us, are functions of a host of conditions and causes, according to science. If we give up belief in contra-causal free will, we're forced to acknowledge that had we been in their circumstances we would have *been* them, holding their beliefs and acting as they do. This insight can help undo the rigid us-versus-them polarization that drives so much violence. Challenging the myth of our supernatural freedom is just what the doctor ordered to help bring the world to its senses.

http://www.naturalism.org/davies.htm

Science and Critical Thinking

Through its allegiance to empiricism, naturalism counters the pseudo-science and magical thinking of New Age mysticism, not to mention astrology, fortune telling and other "psychic" arts. Although proponents of the New Age (for instance gurus such as Ken Wilbur and Andrew Cohen) like to claim scientific backing for paranormal abilities and "conscious evolution," there's no solid, peer-reviewed experimental evidence for occult mental powers or for the idea that human consciousness is evolving toward any goal. Among other things, naturalism is the tough-minded refusal to let our strong desires for meaning and control warp our perception of reality. See Lee Silver's

Challenging Nature for a bracing rebuttal of all manner of fuzzy thinking about the soul and New Age mysticism, and see Michael Shermer's *Why People Believe Weird Things* for an insightful diagnosis of our penchant for irrational beliefs.

There are of course tremendous practical implications in the public domain that follow from taking science, not faith, wishful thinking or rigid ideology as the basis for belief. Effective policies on health and the environment depend directly on science, so it's no exaggeration to say that respect for science is critical for social and planetary survival. The consequences of suppressing and distorting empirical findings, for instance on global warming, are dire indeed. In promoting science and empiricism, naturalists therefore play an unabashedly progressive role in protecting and enhancing the common good. See Chris Mooney's book *The Republican War On Science* for a chilling recent history of attempts by those with vested religious and economic interests to thwart consideration of the best available evidence.

In the educational arena, naturalists will, naturally, want to foster public support and understanding of science and critical thinking. These are essential for evaluating evidence and for appreciating the causal connections that shape our lives, the basis for the applied naturalism explored here. Empirical and skeptical habits of mind, the cognitively responsible trait of subjecting one's beliefs to critical scrutiny – these are essential to combat dogmatic certitudes and to reinforce the norm of open inquiry so essential to democracy. Such habits can be taught from an early age with lessons on thinking skills, basic philosophy (many kids love the big questions), and of course hands-on science. A respect for what grown-ups call rational empiricism can be fostered indirectly by teaching children and adolescents about the "Big Story" of cosmic and human evolution, and how scientists came up with it. Conveying the tremendous, awe-inspiring scale and complexity of the natural world might even inspire a desire to participate in the scientific project itself.

Surveys of religious beliefs show that higher educational levels are associated with holding a more naturalistic worldview. Naturalists should therefore support good non-sectarian public schools that give each child ample opportunity to develop his or her intellectual abilities so that they can, if they wish, continue on to college. Assuring that public schools provide good teachers and a safe, respectful social environment will minimize the attraction of private religious schools, where exposure to unbiased science and critical thinking is often compromised.

As some students will discover, science describes a universe of vast dimensions and myriad forms that can make traditional supernatural conceptions of the world seem limited and parochial by comparison. The grand unity of nature revealed by science – the connections between all levels of phenomena as expressed in physical, chemical and biological laws – is deeply satisfying to those driven to make sense of things. The story of cosmic and biological evolution, as told for instance by Carl Sagan in his TV series *Cosmos*, inspires wonder as profound as any offered by faith. We take for granted the enormous practical benefits conferred by a scientific understanding of cause and effect, but the aesthetic and existential implications of the unity of nature, addressed in the following chapter, are perhaps yet to be fully appreciated.

www.naturalism.org/new_age.htm
www.naturalism.org/science.htm

7

Naturalizing Spirituality

Having surveyed the personal, social, and planetary implications of naturalism, we turn now to the widest possible context, what theologian Paul Tilich called the "ultimate concerns" of human meaning and purpose. Traditionally, such concerns have been the province of supernatural and dualistic religions and spiritual beliefs. These teach that the real meaning of our lives derives from god and his purposes, or perhaps a goal toward which nature itself is heading. But naturalism denies that there's a creator with plans for us, or that nature has a goal in mind (science discerns no such goal as yet), so it denies that our lives can partake of such purposes. Nor, under naturalism, do we have souls that survive death, to join the creator in the hereafter.

This chapter argues that, without god, ultimate purposes or immortal souls, we can nevertheless reconstrue both religious reverence and spirituality in non-supernatural, non-dualist terms; we can *naturalize* spirituality. Appreciating our complete inclusion in the natural world can generate feelings of connection and significance equal to those offered by traditional religions. Indeed, the naturalist sees that such feelings mirror the empirical reality of our immersion in nature. We can seek authentic spiritual experiences of wonder, awe, and reverence, and legitimately describe ourselves as religious, even if we happen to be card-carrying atheists. In the first chapter of his book *The God Delusion*, Richard Dawkins calls this "Einsteinian religion."

To characterize experiences of wonder and connection as *spiri-*

tual, of course, is to risk evoking all the otherworldly, incorporeal connotations traditionally associated with the word. But I use it nevertheless, reclaiming it for naturalism, since apart from its dualistic baggage (which will be decisively rejected in what follows) the term is exactly appropriate to describe our emotional engagement with the deepest questions of our lives.

Spiritual Experience

From a naturalistic perspective, spiritual experience – the profound, direct experience of meaning and connection – is a state of the physical person, not evidence for a higher, non-physical realm. After all, *all* experiences, according to neuroscience, are the brain in action; no "ghost in the machine" or link to a higher reality is necessary to explain them. So feeling transported or deeply connected, the hallmarks of spiritual experience, doesn't imply there's anything immaterial being manifested. Nevertheless, this tough-minded, physicalist understanding of spirituality doesn't lessen the attraction of such an experience or its value for the naturalist. Many of us naturally crave such feelings and will seek them out in the context of our philosophy. Crucially, spiritual experience reflects *our actual situation in the world* as science-based naturalism reveals it. Science and spirituality are therefore mutually consistent, not in conflict.

The Dilemma for Naturalists

But the question for the naturalist arises: how, as someone who doesn't believe in transcendent, otherworldly connections, can I legitimately evoke such feelings? How, consistent with naturalism as my worldview, can I find the same emotional resonance or the same sorts of consolations that my supernaturally inclined friends experience? In short, what is spiritually uplifting about naturalism?

For naturalism to evoke states akin to those evoked by faith-based religion, its precepts must have profound and positive psychological consequences. Its conclusions must resonate with the naturalist's desire for connection and meaning, even though naturalism tends to undercut the presumption of an overarching purpose. What, then, are some of the implications of naturalism for our ultimate concerns?

The Cosmic Connection

Most generally, naturalism places us firmly within the natural realm, extending from quarks to quasars. The scope of this realm as depicted in our sciences is nothing less than staggering. It is a far more varied, complex and vast creation than any provided by faith-based religion, offering an infinite vista of questions to engage us. What naturalism takes away in terms of a central, secure role for us in god's kingdom is more than compensated for by the open-ended excitement of being part of something whose dimensions, purpose and precise nature may never be known. In accepting a naturalistic view of ourselves, we trade security for surprise, certainty for an unending quest for understanding, and easy platitudes about salvation for a flexible, mature accommodation to the often difficult facts of life and death.

That we are alive and sentient, with the capacity to form an understanding of nature, however provisional, is the source of much amazement to the naturalist, since after all, none of our component parts is sentient. Such amazement (and there are thousands of natural facts that evoke it) can be the start of spiritual experience. The stuff of our bodies came originally from the Big Bang, transmuted by stars and expelled in supernovas, and this connects us, literally, to the most far flung corners of the universe, in both space and time. As Chet Raymo puts it in *Skeptics and True Believers*:

To admit that we are matter and mechanism is to ground our selves in the wholeness of the cosmos. In the new physics, self coalesces from the stuff of the stars, exists briefly... then flows back into wholeness. Such a concept of self can be ennobling, cosmic, ecological – more so than the ghostly spirit soul I encountered in freshman theology... To understand that we are structurally no different from the rest of the cosmos is to let ourselves expand into infinity.

This deep sense of connection, of an expanded self derived from contemplating our origins in the cosmos, is a defining characteristic of spirituality.

The aesthetics of nature (which again includes culture) can also play an important role in generating the spiritual response. The raw, undesigned colors of Brazilian agate, the paintings of the Renaissance masters, the grand structure of the Great Wall of galaxies – all are marvels at different scales. The opportunities for amazement afforded by the natural world in its complexity and variety are nearly limitless.

A further inspiration to us, curiously enough, is that nature *can't* be tied up neatly in our understanding: we will always stand astonished at the vastness of its possibilities, knowing that we comprehend just a fraction of what might be known, and knowing that there is no end to it. Faced with all this, the naturalist, if she is capable of letting go into a non-cognitive response, may discover feelings of profound awe and surrender, feelings typical of religious revelation but now felt in a cognitive context of the most hard-edged empiricism. Although it is not widely known, the full appreciation of naturalism and its implications can be as intoxicating, perhaps more so, than any traditional religion. Ursula Goodenough describes letting go in her book on religious naturalism, *The Sacred Depths of Nature*:

The realization that I needn't have answers to the Big Questions, needn't seek answers to the Big Questions has served as an epiphany. I lie on my back under the stars and the unseen galaxies and I let their enormity wash over me. I assimilate the vastness of the distances, the impermanence, the *fact* of it all. I go all the way out and then I go all the way down, to the fact of photons without mass and gauge bosons that become massless at high temperatures. I take in the abstractions about forces and symmetries and they caress me like Gregorian chants, the meaning of the words not mattering because the words are so haunting.

No Ultimate Purpose

It's easy to see that from a naturalistic perspective there cannot be any ultimate purpose to existence: as soon as any purpose is proposed, one can simply ask why *that* purpose should drive existence, as opposed to some other purpose. Even if a god created us to glorify him and his works, we are still creatures that can ask why god himself exists, and why his purposes should be considered ultimate. As questioners, we will always be able to second guess any overarching meaning that someone, even a god, attaches to the universe. Existence is always prior to its interpretation, and the idea of a purpose-endowing creator begs the questions of its *own* origin and *its* purpose for being. In short, our intelligence, if we stay true to it, guarantees that we will never rest secure in a comfortable, pat construal of existence.

The initial psychological response to this dilemma is sometimes the melancholy feeling that life is therefore devoid of meaning. Since we can never construe an ultimate purpose, what's the point, anyway? It's no wonder that in reacting to the specter of purposelessness, people often insist there's got to be *something more* than just space, matter and energy – a driving cosmic intention, perhaps. But once we've understood the unstable logic of the desire for ultimate meaning – that by its very nature it's an unsatisfiable demand – we can begin to savor our position as a very curious one indeed. It turns out that smart creatures like us, if they are honest about their situation, will never be in a position to satisfy themselves about meaning, at least of the ultimate variety.

This discovery, of what we might call the fundamental *inscrutability* of existence, prevents a complacent, boring acceptance of the status quo from ever setting in. There is no particular way things are ultimately *meant* to be, so existence becomes a work in perpetual progress (not toward an intended goal, however), whose outcome is never endorsed, so to speak. We therefore stand perpetually surprised, curious and wondering. We cannot easily set aside our demand for ultimate meaning, since we are predisposed to look for intention in the world around us and therefore in nature as a whole. But if we understand that the demand is inherently unsatisfiable, we find ourselves free to play with existence, or to be its playthings, sometimes. We create *local* meaning in activities we find intrinsically satisfying; we get completely caught up in our human drama, knowing that the drama is set on a much larger stage whose dimensions may never be known, and which exists for no obvious reason.

Understanding that we're temporary players on the stage makes the spectacle all the more compelling. Were we immortal souls, life would arguably lose a good deal of its urgency and value – think of plastic flowers: virtually indestructible but aesthetically empty. Impermanence, not permanence, is what most drives our engagement in life.

The direct appreciation of the inscrutability of existence, letting go of the need for an ultimate purpose, can have a profound and positive psychological impact: we are free of the deadening certainty that we have a prescribed role to play and a "correct" goal to achieve. Not being the servants of god, we gain in autonomy. We are liberated to be perpetually amazed at the sheer, startling fact that something exists, not nothing, and that we are integral parts of it.

Experiences of awe, astonishment, rapture and connection are central aspects of spirituality that naturalism affords us. When contemplating the widest context of human existence, naturalists are therefore at no disadvantage compared to traditional religionists. Indeed, the empirical truth generated by science works quite wonderfully to ground and inspire our approach to ultimate concerns.

www.naturalism.org/spiritua.htm
www.naturalim.org/death.htm

8

Naturalism, Supernaturalism and the Culture Wars

The conflict between naturalism and supernaturalism is at the heart of many disagreements about fundamental facts and values in what's popularly known as the culture wars. As the fierce debates testify, no easy reconciliation is forthcoming between the traditional, dualistic view of ourselves as embodied souls and the science-based view that we are completely natural creatures. In many cases, naturalism supports the more progressive, liberal side in these debates. This is emphatically *not* to say, however, that all naturalists are progressive, or that naturalism is the only source of progressive values. In seeking a more humane, equitable and flourishing society, humanistic naturalists should make common cause with others who share their goals, whatever their worldview.

Is Being Gay a Choice?

The religious right often claims that the gay "lifestyle" is an individual's choice, a voluntary decision to willfully flout the natural order created by god, and thus a moral failing. On the other side, naturalists who accept the findings of science argue that there is a significant genetic component to homosexuality. Further, they argue, because it isn't the intentional creation of a homophobic god, the natural order doesn't establish the intrinsic inferiority of homosexual behavior.

So the question is: do we shape ourselves through acts of pure free will to conform to god's wishes, or do we explain ourselves as a matter of causal influences in an unauthored universe? If it's the former, then gays are themselves to blame for an immoral, freely willed choice and thus deserve their status as second class citizens without equal rights, for instance to marry. If it's the latter, then we can see homosexuality as a fully caused, morally neutral aspect of the natural world, not a violation of god's will, in which case there's no good reason to discriminate against gays.

The burden on those wanting to limit gay rights is to show what harm there is in being gay or in permitting gays to marry. Absent religiously motivated claims about the moral depravity of homosexuality, there are no demonstrable harms in being gay or any threats to society from gay marriage. It's clear, then, that the naturalistic understanding of homosexuality is inherently progressive, since it sees no obstacle to gays being accepted as full-fledged, rights-bearing members of society. Such acceptance, like the emancipation of slaves and women's suffrage, counts as moral progress.

www.naturalism.org/sexualit.htm

Abortion, Stem Cells, and the Soul

Policy advocacy on abortion and embryonic stem cell research is often driven by conflicting beliefs about personhood and the sanctity of life. If you believe that an embryo is "ensouled' immediately after conception, then it constitutes a god-created person and must be preserved at nearly any cost, possibly including the health of the mother. Abortion, as well as research involving the deliberate creation and destruction of human embryos, should therefore be prohibited. But if you believe we don't possess souls, then personhood might come later. Abortion and stem cell research might well be permissible, depending on the needs, desires and rights of actual persons.

These disputes involve two very different notions of what's central and valuable about being human, one *essentialist* and supernatural, the other *emergentist* and naturalistic. The former holds that what's most valuable about a person is the indivisible and essential core that's present from conception – the immaterial soul. The latter holds that the value of an individual human being, both for itself and as felt by others, derives from having characteristics such as consciousness, personality, desires and self-interests that *emerge* from complex physical processes. Since these characteristics of personhood are not present at the earliest stages of life in the womb (the complex processes supporting them aren't in place yet), those stages generally don't elicit the same concern and thus don't motivate the same legal protection accorded to fully-formed persons. Abortion is therefore permissible until the stage of pregnancy at which we decide a fetus *is* a person. Since people have different intuitions about the onset of personhood, that decision, at least as expressed in law, is inevitably political.

A naturalistic understanding of personhood doesn't involve any religious or non-empirical belief, such as the conviction that the soul gets installed at conception by god. It's therefore closely aligned with the commonly held *secular* definition of a person that's reflected in current law. States allow (sometimes reluctantly) a woman to terminate her pregnancy before the third trimester, so clearly the current legal consensus in the US is that embryos and early-stage fetuses are *not* persons with an overriding right to life. The closer a fetus is to a newborn baby in characteristics and capacities, the more likely we are to consider it a person, and by the 3rd trimester many believe a person is present. Still, anti-abortion advocates, often motivated by belief in the supernatural soul, are working hard to prohibit abortion from conception onward.

Here again the conflict between naturalism and supernaturalism is at the root of an ongoing battle in the culture wars. As a naturalistic view of ourselves prevails, so too will a woman's right to choose an abortion gain protection. Similarly, government support for embryonic stem cell research will become less controversial as belief in the soul declines. See Peter Wenz's *Abortion Rights as Religious Freedom* for a well-argued defense of abortion rights on constitutional grounds of church-state separation.

www.naturalism.org/abortion.htm

Death and Dignity

The debate over death and dignity, played out in the notorious Terri Schiavo case and Oregon's law permitting physician-assisted dying, involves the conflict between two very different conceptions of existence and purpose. From a naturalistic standpoint, the human lifespan is a matter of evolutionary contingency, not an expression of any plan or intention. Although we've been "designed" by nature to want to live, the requirement that we *must* continue living, whatever the quality of our lives, isn't anywhere ordained or endorsed by nature. Taken as a whole, nature intends and desires nothing. This means when it comes to end of life decisions, the naturalist sees no externally imposed obligation to live. The decision about when to die should ultimately rest with her desires and values, with all necessary safeguards to make sure she decides sanely, voluntarily, and without coercion.

This of course contrasts with the beliefs of many religionists, who feel that to take control of dying is to usurp what god has ordained as the proper trajectory of life. We're allowed to intentionally *prolong* life since life is sacred, but not to intentionally end it, whatever suffering or indignity we might have to endure. The individual must sacrifice her interests to the greater good of conforming to god's purposes.

The supernaturalist view therefore negates individual autonomy while the naturalist view supports it. By denying the divine mandate to live, naturalism reinforces the value of self-determination and personal freedom which includes, finally, the freedom to choose death over life. Ideally, such a choice would be carried out with dignity, without pain or dread, in possession of one's faculties and with the loving support of one's family, friends and peers. To draw life to a close intentionally and aesthetically – this is perhaps the capstone of a life well lived.

Although palliative terminal care in hospices is widely available, most of us don't yet have the legal means or opportunity to arrange our deaths to be conscious, intentional and dignified. We have to wait till the body finally fails, or until pain-relieving drugs do their "secondary" work of inducing death, or we must take matters privately into our own hands, often incompetently and brutally. The presumption that life must be lived to the organic end still trumps individual autonomy, reinforced by the religious belief that sheer continued existence is sacred. As naturalism takes hold and calls that belief into question, we will grant ourselves the liberty to die with dignity at a time of our choosing, with the compassionate, legal assistance of those we trust.

www.naturalism.org/death.htm

The Evolution Wars

When understood as the conflict between naturalism and supernaturalism, the culture wars are perhaps best epitomized by the debate over teaching evolution in public schools. Those sympathetic to creationism and intelligent design sometimes claim that because science doesn't consider supernatural causes when explaining evolution it therefore promotes naturalism. Scientists and science teachers reply that, sorry, the scientific method of explanation necessarily rules out the supernatural. Why? Because the supernatural is that which by definition can't be shown to interact with, and thus explain, natural phenomena. Anything science discovers that helps to explain how species evolve would of necessity be incorporated into our unified understanding of the world, and so would become part of nature and thus *not* supernatural. So science doesn't presume or promote naturalism – the denial of the supernatural; it's just that the world it describes and explains is necessarily the natural world.

The problem for proponents of intelligent design, of course, is that the theory of natural selection Darwin came up with doesn't involve a supernatural, intelligent agent. Evolution can be accounted for by the operation of *un*intelligent, non-purposive mechanisms (see Dawkin's *The Blind Watchmaker* and Dennett's *Darwin's Dangerous Idea*). As the intelligent designer is rendered superfluous in explaining life, there's less and less reason to believe it exists. It's no wonder, then, that although it doesn't presume naturalism, science is perceived as a threat to faith-based religion. It makes a naturalistic view of the world more, shall we say, natural.

www.naturalism.org/science.htm

Self-Control and the Role of Government

Attitudes about behavioral health, such as mental illness, addiction and obesity, are often shaped by underlying beliefs about the self and its freedom. One side, usually more conservative, says that persons have free will and should be able to snap out of their depression; they should *just choose* to stop over-eating, drinking, smoking and gambling. The emphasis is on "personal responsibility" for achieving self-control and making healthy choices, not treatment and social policy. The other side, usually more liberal, believes people often need help with these problems, so why not prevent and treat behavioral disorders the way we do other diseases? Why shouldn't the state play a role in fostering healthy behavior and encouraging wise choices? Self-control and mental health are achieved not through the miracle of free will, but through education, environments, and policies that permit optimal development and that provide help when things go wrong.

These two very different ideas about willpower and self-control underlie arguments about the role of government. If people are capable of simply *choosing* to exert self-control then they don't need help, and if they fail to control themselves it's basically their fault. This view puts all responsibility on the individual, letting the state and the rest of us off the hook. This is, of course, the perfect rationale for small government libertarian conservatism, hence the right's affection for the idea of *personal* responsibility. On the other hand, if one's capacity for self-control isn't a matter of contra-causal free will but is instead caused by various factors (e.g., parental modeling of responsible behavior and consistent rules in schools and communities) then responsibility for self-control is *distributed outside the individual*.

Recognizing this, we might be more proactive in creating home, school and community environments in which children learn effective self-management techniques. And if we accept that choices about eating, drinking, smoking and gambling are a function of external temptations as well as individual discipline, that's a good reason to adopt policies of *public* self-management, for instance regulations that limit the advertising and availability of junk food, cigarettes and slot machines. Similarly, seeing that mental illnesses such as depression and obsessive-compulsive disorder aren't self-chosen character flaws, but syndromes traceable to neurological and environmental conditions, should prompt us to prevent these conditions when possible and offer treatment when prevention fails.

This debate about self-control and the role of government – fac-

ets of the culture wars – hinges considerably on ideas about the metaphysics of human nature. Naturalism, based in a scientific view of human beings as fully caused creatures, suggests that we have a shared
responsibility to create the conditions in which people can learn and
exert self-control and make good, productive choices.

www.naturalism.org/maximizing_liberty.htm
www.naturalism.addictio.htm

Crime and Human Nature

Speaking to an audience of police officers, New York governor George
Pataki, a staunch conservative, once opined that the root cause of
crime is criminals. Criminals create themselves, essentially, so the
idea that external circumstances play a role in crime is simply to excuse bad behavior. Liberals, on the other hand, are notoriously more
likely to focus on the *determinants* of the criminal: unhealthy family
and community environments that sometimes interact with inherited
susceptibilities to conduct disorders. Attitudes about criminal justice
reflect these opposite assumptions about human nature. Conservatives are more likely to emphasize that punishment is deserved for
willful misbehavior, so don't coddle the criminal. Liberals advocate
understanding him the better to rehabilitate him and prevent others
from following in his footsteps.

The more punitive conservative approach, based partially in the
free will assumption, has largely carried the day. But with the rise of
neuroscience the idea of contra-causal free will is under considerable
pressure. If, as science tends to show, criminals don't create themselves, this undercuts the conservative laissez-faire approach to criminality. Instead, perhaps we should get *smart* on crime and take into
account the causal story behind the offender. Our heavy reliance on
punishment might give way to a social-behavioral systems approach

that emphasizes effective prevention and rehabilitation. In the war of ideas about crime, naturalism suggests we should be *intentional* in addressing what causes criminals and stop being merely punitive.

This isn't to say that when it comes to crime or any other aspect of human behavior conservatives always ignore causes, or that liberals don't have significant blind spots about causality (they tend to downplay genetic factors, for instance). Indeed, one argument in the culture wars is about exactly this: which side best grasps the realities of human nature and social dynamics? This is a healthy debate since it keeps both sides honest and establishes common ground, namely that we should be responsive to the empirical facts. Naturalists are committed to respecting the evidence, wherever it leads, so as naturalism makes headway we can hope for more reality-based discourse in the culture wars.

www.naturalism.org/criminal.htm

Naturalism and the Open Society

As heated as the culture wars may be, they are actually characteristic of a healthy, open society, in which ideas are debated, not literally fought over. Keeping society open, as opposed to authoritarian, is a fundamental value, and naturalism is by nature friendly to democracy and free debate. Because it's premised on a commitment to rational empiricism, naturalism keeps our focus on the observable physical and social world here on Earth, not the unobservable supernatural world to come, should it exist. It therefore isn't ideological and divisive in the way that many non-empirical worldviews are: clinging to a fixed understanding no matter what the contrary evidence. Likewise, naturalists aren't defensive or self-righteous about naturalism, or at least they shouldn't be. They acknowledge our cognitive fallibility, that our view of reality might stand improvement. It is through unfettered debate and gathering evidence, not by imposing an ideology, that our understanding of the world becomes more accurate and thus more effective. A commitment to these cognitive virtues translates directly into support for an open society.

In a diverse, democratic society where there are conflicting ideas about ultimate reality, it's vital that there be agreement about our shared *present* reality. We have a cognitive responsibility to one another – an ethical obligation – to hold well-justified, reliable beliefs about the world we have in common, for instance about global warming, avian flu and the causes of genocide. It's science and evidence-based rationality that allow this. Naturalism, not supernaturalism, is committed to empiricism and thus champions the creation of a *cognitive common ground* which multi-cultural societies depend upon to flourish. Since this common ground depends on the free exchange of ideas and information, naturalists are naturally and strongly motivated to keep society open.

On the other hand, once authoritarian, non-empirical religions and political ideologies take over, the prospects for an open society diminish rapidly. The quest for ideological conformity, often inspired by absolutist thinking, can involve the violent suppression of opposing views, as for example in the international jihad of some extreme Islamists. Of course, *non-religious* jihads that champion decidedly unscientific, non-empirical understandings of human nature and history – white supremacy, Nazism, the inevitable triumph of the proletariat – have been mounted as well, with horrific consequences. Hence the importance of preventing the imposition of a single conception of ultimate reality – not even naturalism! – on citizens who should be thinking for themselves. This will help keep the culture wars a non-violent conflict of ideas, not arms.

www.naturalism.org/culture_wars.htm

9

The Prospects for Naturalism

This book has outlined some virtues of an explicit, positive naturalism, a philosophy that places us securely in the natural world. The significance of naturalism lies in its profound redefinition of who we are and the consequences of that redefinition for ourselves and society. We are no longer souls that happen to have bodies; instead, we are fully physical creatures whose brains do everything the soul was supposed to do. In declaring our complete causal connection to nature, naturalism shows us to be at home in the cosmos. We are what the universe is doing here and now in this particular human configuration, and, thanks to science, we can trace our lineage back through the eons to the Big Bang. Seeing our causal origins in genetics and the environment, and understanding that persons and society are unfolding natural processes, traditional beliefs about the self, freedom, moral agency, and credit and blame are called into question. Knowing that we are not self-created or first causes, we might take a more compassionate view of ourselves and others. Using the knowledge science gives us about ourselves, we might become more effective in our personal lives, relationships and work. Naturalism also supports enlightened and effective social policies in many domains and is friendly to democratic ideals. Finally, it can ground an intellectually respectable and emotionally satisfying approach to ultimate concerns of meaning and purpose. So, what's not to like?

Reassurances

Well, despite these virtues, a big question looms about the acceptabil-
ity of naturalism. After all, it challenges central assumptions in Western culture about the basis for knowledge (science, not faith), the nature of existence (a single natural world, no god or the supernatural)
and the nature of the self (we are brains and bodies, not souls). For
the current majority not committed to science as a way of deciding
about ultimate reality, naturalism stands as a threat to some dearly
cherished notions of human agency, ethics and meaning. Without
having god to watch over us, a soul to survive death, and free will to
choose independently of antecedent conditions, life might seem pretty bleak, human prospects vastly diminished. We are not self-made
selves who deserve ultimate credit and blame, nor are we at the center
of any grand cosmic plan, nor is there "something more" beyond the
physical world that grounds morality or gives life a purpose.

For many, these are bitter pills indeed, but the disappointment
of self-centered human hope is hardly unprecedented. Based in modern science, naturalism is the culmination of the Copernican and
Darwinian revolutions, both of which sparked fierce resistance as
they pushed us off the pedestal of cosmic centrality. The response to
naturalism is likely to include heated denials that science has the final
say about who we are, and a more fervid embrace of non-empirical
worldviews that promise such things as eternal life and supernatural foundations for ethics. Science might be acceptable as a practical
tool, but not as the basis for a worldview.

So it seems that advocates of naturalism have their work cut
out for them. To make naturalism palatable, naturalists have to provide reassurances, as for instance in Appendix A. We have to show
the world doesn't end once we give up the supernatural. We are still
moral agents, we can still be held (compassionately) responsible, and
we can still find meaning in life. We retain our real freedom and

dignity, and we continue to love and value ourselves and others. We remain rational, effective agents (perhaps more effective, actually), whose choices make a real difference in the world. In short, we must show that we lose nothing of value in embracing naturalism, unless someone's attached to the supernatural basis for pride and contempt (contra-causal free will) or wants to remain ignorant of what makes us who we are (by chalking up behavior to the self-caused self).

To gain acceptance for naturalism we must also develop its detailed, concrete applications to relationships, work, society and the planet, some of which I've sketched above. The progressive implications and consequences of naturalism will have broad appeal once people understand that they don't threaten our values or self-efficacy.

We may not be at the center of things, according to naturalism, but we are fully *part* of things, and to accept this is to achieve maturity as a species, to take our place in nature. The advent of naturalism can be understood, and welcomed, as our *coming of age*.

Modeling Personal Virtues

In living up to their worldview, naturalists will do their best to model the empathy, compassion and acceptance that flow from understanding our caused, interdependent nature. Not that we're push-overs, but we'll respond less reactively and thoughtlessly to provocations. We won't suppose we're morally superior than those less lucky in life, and we'll take their causal story into account in judging them: there but for circumstances go I. We'll also be more mindful of the factors that affect us and others, that determine our choices and behavior. This should make us smarter in creating the conditions that produce good choices and that help us to lead balanced, productive lives. Compassion, rooted in our understanding of causality, is matched by the increased control conferred by understanding the factors that shape us. To the extent we can successfully live out the implications of naturalism in our own lives, we'll gain the respect and trust of those who worry that naturalism might undermine personal virtues.

Do We Really Need Another "Ism"?

Some of those skeptical about faith-based religions and other non-empirical belief systems are equally skeptical about whole-heartedly endorsing *any* worldview. They don't particularly want to sign on to another "ism," something which might be, or turn into, a fixed creed or ideology. Or perhaps as staunchly independent thinkers they don't want to be pinned down or pigeonholed – no labels on *me*, thank you very much. Although they might endorse a rational, empirical approach to justifying beliefs, and not have any truck with the supernatural, they balk at describing themselves as naturalists.

Fair enough. The skeptical, independent habit of mind underlying this refusal is exactly the cognitive virtue that naturalism encourages. And indeed, those suspicious of naturalism as an ism – a potentially restrictive ideology – are welcome to expose it as such. If naturalism can be shown defective, for instance in imposing cognitive blinders, limiting the range of human experience, or blunting our engagement with the world and each other, then it must yield to whatever worldview does better.

Absent this critique, however, those who are naturalists in all but name might consider coming out as such (although the counter-suggestible among them likely won't). Atheists, secular humanists, skeptics and freethinkers are all essentially naturalistic in their worldview, even if it isn't always explicitly acknowledged. Naturalism simply names this worldview, naturalists are simply those that subscribe to it.

To count yourself a *thorough-going* naturalist is, however, to go beyond what many atheists, humanists and skeptics are currently willing to accept. Denying god is fine, but denying contra-causal free will? That's a real problem for many. Nor will the progressive implications of a thorough-going naturalism be particularly palatable to secular conservatives. If they consider themselves true-blue naturalists, they must either deny there are progressive implications of accepting that we're fully caused beings, or formulate a naturalized notion of contra-causal freedom (very difficult!). Such critiques are welcome since naturalism is by definition based on open inquiry.

But again, do we really need another ism, in this case naturalism? Well, if it's an accurate, convenient label for what you believe on careful consideration to be the case, make use of it. Not to name your worldview, after all, leaves it at a competitive disadvantage in the marketplace of belief, what Susan Blackmore, author of *The Meme Machine*, would call the "meme-o-sphere."

Cultural Momentum

Even if it's a tough sell in some ways, naturalism has its own growing momentum propelled by the rise of science. Naturalistic explanations of phenomena have gradually replaced or challenged supernatural explanations. This process will likely continue into the domain of human behavior, putting increasing pressure on traditional notions of the self and its freedom. Should science and empiricism win greater acceptance, so too will naturalism. After all, it's the logical, most consistent position to take once we decide that evidence-based beliefs should be our guide to reality. Many people are, practically speaking, naturalists in most aspects of their lives, since they want good evidence when deciding day-to-day factual questions. The increasingly visible debates about neuroscience and the soul, criminal justice and causality, determinism and moral responsibility and the like, simply extend this commonsense empiricism to the big questions of life; they point to the conclusion that humans are, ultimately, no exception to the causal order. As our self-knowledge grows, so too will the plausibility of naturalism.

Of course, there's no historical inevitability about this process. Allegiance to science and empirical justifications for belief are cultural constructions that could disappear rather rapidly under the right conditions, such as a successful global religious jihad. So the propagation of naturalism must be an intentional project, one that actively defends the values of empirical inquiry, critical thinking, open debate, freedom of conscience, and the equal right of all individuals to participate in shaping society. The fate of naturalism and the fate of democratic, secular culture might well be inextricably linked.

If the naturalism you've encountered here seems a viable worldview, I invite your participation in making it known and developing its applications. Naturalism is a reality-based, humanistic and effective philosophy of life that can see us safely through the 21st century, and into the world to come.

Appendix A
Concerns and Reassurances

When people first encounter naturalism, especially as it applies to ourselves and our place in the world, it can engender a good deal of defensiveness, and no wonder: the applecart of traditional assumptions about the self, free will, responsibility, meaning, and a host of other issues is substantially upset. People don't particularly like to hear, as Tom Wolfe put it in an article for *Forbes*, that "Sorry, but your soul just died." So they understandably reach for the nearest rebuttal at hand, usually involving some sort of social or personal value that simply *must* trump the claims of naturalism. For example: "If we didn't have free will then we'd be robots, so we *do* have free will." You might call this the argument from dire consequences, but of course it proves nothing about naturalism.

On the other hand, those who embrace naturalism, discovering in it a satisfying, coherent and useful worldview, sometimes draw conclusions that overreach or distort the naturalistic facts of the matter. Some things change if we accept naturalism, but certainly not everything. Human persons, for instance, don't stop being real entities that figure importantly in the unfolding of events. Nor, because human actions are (likely) fully caused, is everything automatically forgiven. Even though some imagine it to be, naturalism is not, to use philosopher Daniel Dennett's phrase, a "universal acid" that dissolves all justifications for our moral practices.

In this appendix, I want to disarm some common concerns and

correct mistakes that often arise when encountering naturalism. If people fall into error (whichever side of the debate they're on), the truth about naturalism and its personal and social implications will be obscured and its value as a worldview compromised. Unless we state clearly the conclusions that follow from naturalism and those that *don't*, a good deal of unnecessary backlash will be generated. Naturalism is true, if we hold to science and empiricism, but we have to get it right (not that what follows is the last word, by any means). Some of the points made below are mentioned in the chapters above, but they bear repeating under separate headings for quick reference. Further details are added in many cases.

Fatalism

Many imagine that if we don't have some sort of contra-causal "leverage" over nature, for instance by virtue of being able to cause things to happen without ourselves being completely caused, then we fall into fatalism. Naturalism denies that we have this sort of leverage since it holds that everything about us, including our capacities for memory, anticipation, thought, deliberation and planning, ultimately comes from somewhere else via our genes or our environment or both. The moment-to-moment expression of these capacities, including our conscious thoughts and actions, and indeed our very selves in every respect, are fully caused phenomena. Assuming this is right, do we then fall prey to fatalism?

Fatalism is the idea that *no matter what one did*, one's fate would have been the same. Because everything is determined, human actions don't really affect outcomes, so it's pointless to exert ourselves in thinking, planning, deliberating and choosing. But it should be clear that this isn't true. Even though our actions are caused, that doesn't mean they don't have effects. It simply isn't the case that no matter what *we* did, the future would have happened as *it* did. Without making efforts we don't get what we want, therefore the future we want *depends on us* to a great extent. So naturalism does not entail fatalism. However, giving up the myth of contra-causal free will entails thinking quite differently about ourselves and our relationship to the world.

www.naturalism.org/fatalism.htm

Personal Agency and Power

Closely related to the fear of fatalism is the worry that unless human agents are causally disconnected from prior circumstances, then we can't claim that people really *do* anything; we can't consider them to be real agents. If people are determined, through and through, then they are simply the "working out" of causality and contribute nothing to the world. As philosopher Saul Smilansky puts it in "Free Will, Fundamental Dualism, and the Centrality of Illusion" in Robert Kane's book *The Oxford Handbook of Free Will*: "…her decisions, that which is most truly her own, appear to be accidental phenomena of which she is the mere vehicle." For Smilansky, naturalism implies we don't really have causal powers of our *own*. But is this true?

In the natural world, where all is subject to cause and effect, we can nevertheless distinguish various entities with identifiable boundaries marking them off from their surroundings. Human beings are one class of such entities, and persons are separate individuals, each with his or her own set of traits and characteristics. As a particular individual, a person produces effects on the world that can be produced in no other way. Indeed, no two people produce just the same effects, even in similar situations.

This means that persons are necessarily crucial elements in telling causal stories about the world. We can't understand or explain our world without referring to the causal powers, rational capacities and actions of persons. Nor are we in a position to explain or understand human behavior without referring to the *reasons* people have for acting – their goals and motives. People can't be understood at the sub-personal level of chemicals and neurons and organs, at least not for most of our social and interpersonal purposes. So even if persons are determined in all respects, we can't conclude that they don't exist, contribute nothing to the world, and have no causal powers. They have *considerable* powers that only human individuals have, for instance to build societies, create works of art and explore the universe. Furthermore, being undetermined would add nothing to personal self-efficacy, only insert an element of randomness. In his book *The Robot's Rebellion*, Keith Stanovich presents an original, scientifically informed account of how human beings, as naturally evolved, fully caused creatures, can best realize their (proximate, not ultimate) autonomy.

Passivity, Victimhood and Excuses

A further worry generated by the idea of our complete immersion in causality is that we are, or might become, passive onlookers of life. Some think that unless we are first causes we are necessarily "victims of circumstance." Believing this, we might become complacent, letting ourselves completely off the hook for our mistakes. What, me worry? After all, your honor, I was completely caused to do it, wasn't I?

True, you're caused in each and every respect, but if you behave badly or fail to live up to expectations (yours and others'), you still have good reasons to feel regret and to want to do better next time. If you have a conscience, standards, and goals (and it's likely you do), these provide powerful reasons which ensure that you'll be *caused* not to become passive or claim victimhood in the face of determinism.

Understanding the causal story of failing to do the right thing gives you information you can use to do better next time; but that there *is* such a story isn't a good reason to give up your conscience, goals or standards.

Those tempted by the "universal excuse" of causality can be warned as follows: *if* you let yourself off the hook, ceasing to feel any regret or holding yourself to any standards just because you were caused to fail, *then* you won't like the consequences. Expect to be shunned and distrusted, seen as a shirker and non-cooperator. Passivity and claiming victimhood won't get you far, and for good reason: you have causal powers and the failure to use them to do better next time gets you a bad reputation, which of course you don't want. Seeing the consequences of playing the victim will prevent you from claiming victimhood, by giving you a good reason not to.

The proper conclusion about all this is simply to acknowledge that, yes, our genetic and environmental circumstances make us who we are, but we often play, and should play, *active* roles in life. We often act purposefully to fulfill plans and desires (applying to college), even if sometimes we end up as passive victims of events well beyond our control (getting hit by a drunk driver). To suppose that even when we're actively pursuing our goals we're merely puppets of determinism is to ignore a real distinction between agenthood and victimhood, a distinction that lies within an overarching causality. Naturalism doesn't erase this distinction, but simply shows we don't need to be supernatural agents in order to be, a good deal of the time, active, responsible participants in the world. As University of Pennsylvania law professor Stephen Morse put it so wonderfully: "We can't wait for determinism to happen" ("Reason, Results, and Criminal Responsibility," *University of Illinois Law Review* 2: 363–444, 2004).

Real Choices

Not having contra-causal free will seems to have the disturbing implication that people don't make real choices. To have a *real* choice, the chooser mustn't be fully caused to choose the way she did, otherwise what would be the point of choosing and deciding? The naturalistic response to this worry, much like the response to fatalism above, is to remind ourselves that the phenomena of human choosing and deciding are essential elements of the causal process of getting what we want. There's a fantastically complex set of neural algorithms involved in deliberating about the future, a weighing of alternatives in the light of anticipated outcomes, and that process is just as *real* as any other process in nature. Without engaging in it, for instance in deciding what school to attend or what job to accept, you'd simply cease to function effectively. That the process is very likely fully determined doesn't make it any less essential to human flourishing. We don't dismiss the operations of our hearts and spinal cords as being unreal or ineffective because they are deterministic, so why would we for our higher cognitive functions? In his book *Good and Real*, Gary Drescher speaks to this point:

> Thus choice…is a mechanical process compatible with determinism: choice is a process of examining assertions about what would be the case if this or that action were taken, and then selecting an action according to a preference about what would be the case. The objection *The agent didn't really make a choice, because the outcome was already predetermined* is as much a non sequitur as the objection *The motor didn't really exert force, because the outcome was already predetermined…* Both choice making and motor spinning are particular kinds of mechanical processes. In neither case does the predetermination of the outcome imply that the process didn't really take place. (p. 192, original emphasis)

Further, we really don't want random, indeterministic factors to play an important role in the operations of our bodies and brains, since that would make them less dependable. Nor would we want our thinking and deliberative capacities to be indeterministic; if they were, our decisions wouldn't reliably reflect our knowledge and desires. Similarly, we want accurate evidence and information about the world, and it's deterministic, not indeterministic, perceptual and cognitive processes that confer accuracy. And think: if there were some undetermined aspect of yourself that had the final say about what to choose, *on what basis* would it make the decision? Since it isn't being influenced by anything, it has no reason to go left or right, to choose Yale over Dartmouth, or prefer chocolate to vanilla. An undetermined decider behind the choice-making machinery of your brain wouldn't do you any good. *Real* choices, therefore, are what you make day in, day out, as a fully functioning, fully caused, physical creature, negotiating its way in the world. You can't help but make them.

Responsibility

One of the most acute and widespread fears engendered by naturalism is that if all is caused, we can't be held responsible. If someone really and truly couldn't have done other than what he did in the situation in which the behavior arose, then what happens to praise and blame? If people don't originate their actions in some ultimate sense, then how can they be held accountable for their wrongdoings, and why should we reward them for their virtues?

As mentioned in Chapter 3 in the section "Responsibility without free will," two basic points make up the reply to this worry. First, it's clear that even in an entirely deterministic world we would still retain our strong desires for certain basic outcomes, namely the well-being of ourselves and our loved ones. Therefore, we'd still be strongly inclined to protect ourselves and to shape and guide behavior in the directions we want. So the reasons we have for maintaining public safety and a flourishing society would still apply, even if it turns out we're fully caused beings.

Second, being motivated in this way means that we have *good reasons* to hold persons accountable for wrongful, damaging behavior and to reward them for behavior we want encouraged. Such accountability and encouragement are essential to keep behavior within acceptable limits and to create human beings who behave responsibly, considerately and ethically. So even if people don't have contra-causal free will, we still have adequate justifications for keeping dangerous individuals out of society, for imposing sanctions as deterrents, and for other responses to criminality and immorality which will promote social stability and human flourishing. Likewise, we still have good reasons for praising and otherwise rewarding individuals for good behavior, although we won't any longer suppose that they are good because of some uncaused, self-chosen virtue. Without getting such rewards, people simply aren't as motivated to behave as well as they otherwise would.

The upshot is that, under naturalism, many social practices which produce good behavior and protect society are left untouched, even though the justifications for them no longer include the idea that people are uncaused agents deserving of ultimate credit or blame. We must still hold people responsible, even though they are fully caused, since holding them responsible is an important means to *make* them responsible, considerate and ethical. But, since persons can no longer be seen as first causes, we can't any longer suppose that they deserve to suffer or flourish for having simply chosen, independent of circumstances, to act the way they did. This means our responsibility and accountability practices should be as compassionate and non-punitive as possible, informed by what works best to create ethical, considerate human beings.

Moral Standards

Some fear that naturalism, by showing that our values derive only from human nature and culture, invalidates any binding justification for our moral practices. If there's no basis outside of our contingent biological and social situation for what we believe is just, right and good, then how do we make the case for our ethical standards? Although this question gets us into deep waters very quickly, some reassurance can be found in the fact that basic human values are widely shared by virtue of being rooted in our common evolved nature. Scientists such as Franz de Waal (*Good Natured*) and Marc Hauser (*Moral Minds*) are documenting the evolutionary history of our moral sense and have discovered its precursors among the great apes – chimpanzees, bonobos and gorillas.

Each of us has deeply held desires for how we want ourselves and our loved ones to be treated, desires that define the core of everyday morality nearly everywhere we look. There's an innate motivational predisposition for morality stemming from the survival advantage conferred by living in stable groups, which requires cooperation, sharing, reciprocity and forming close attachments to others. Since cooperative individuals forming stable groups were more likely to reproduce (the group protected them) they passed on cooperative predispositions to their descendents – us. We can therefore understand the set of moral attitudes directed at the self and others (shame, pride, guilt, resentment, gratitude, trust, affection) as a natural phenomenon, which in turn explains our strong intuitions about how we *should* treat others and how others *should* treat us. We need not appeal to a supernatural standard of ethical conduct to know that in general it's wrong to lie, cheat, steal, rape, murder, torture, or otherwise treat people in ways we'd rather not be treated. Empathetic concern for others and the Golden Rule of reciprocity get us what we most want as social creatures: to flourish as individuals within a community.

The tougher question for the naturalist (or for anyone, for that matter) is how to justify moral norms and practices specific to cultures, since these obviously differ from place to place. From a naturalistic perspective, norms and practices (e.g., female circumcision, banning the death penalty) can be understood as the contingent outcome of cultural developments, not better or worse approximations to some external moral standard that exists independently of human nature and society. Nevertheless, specific social practices can be evaluated on the basis of whether they are consonant with fundamental human needs and wants – the desires for food, shelter, companionship and freedom, to avoid unnecessary suffering, and to find pleasure and meaningful activities in life. Naturalism may show the ultimate contingency of some values, in that human nature might have evolved differently and human societies and political arrangements might have turned out otherwise. But, given who and what we are as natural creatures, we necessarily find ourselves with shared basic values which serve as the criteria for assessing moral dilemmas, even if these assessments are sometimes fiercely contested and never quite resolved.

For good discussions of how morality might be naturalized see Owen Flanagan's book *The Problem of the Soul*, the chapter entitled "Ethics as Human Ecology," William Casebeer's *Natural Ethical Facts*, Marc Hauser's *Moral Minds*, Franz De Waal's *Good Natured*, Matt Ridley's *The Origins of Virtue* and Robert Wright's *The Moral Animal*. See the last chapters of Gary Drescher's cutting edge *Good and Real* for a mind-bending account of why rational creatures living in a (likely) deterministic universe should obey the Golden Rule.

www.naturalism.org/morality.htm

Individuality

Some take the denial of contra-causal freedom as an affront to human uniqueness or individuality. If we are not ultimately our own creations, then we are less than true individuals. But this claim is a patent non-sequitur. Differences that define your uniqueness as a person arise as a function of your contingent place in time and space; they need not arise by virtue of some self-originating capacity. It's only the Western myth of radical individualism – that persons somehow bootstrap themselves into their individuality – that leads us to suppose uniqueness requires self-origination. The unimaginably vast concatenation of causes that intersect to produce each of us suffices to render every person this *particular* version of *homo sapiens*, the one with just *this* set of attributes and proclivities. Of course, what makes us special as a species is the extent to which our personalities and goals are mediated by complex cognitive processes carried in our heads. In this respect, we are proximately self-authoring. But we don't need to be *ultimately* self-authoring to become unique individuals. B.F. Skinner makes this point in *About Behaviorism*, published in 1974:

> Nothing about the position taken in this book questions the uniqueness of each member of the human species, but the uniqueness is inherent in the sources. There is no place in the scientific position for a self as a true originator or initiator of action.

Novelty and Progress

A closely related misunderstanding is the idea that if all is determined (at the macro level of human-scale concerns), then nothing new really happens under the sun. But far from being banned by determinism, novelty is instead pretty much the norm. Change is possible, indeed inevitable, and sometimes change counts as progress.

Since our cognitive capacities are obviously limited, we are not in a position to predict the future in any detail, determined though it might be, so we're routinely surprised by the way events unfold. As philosophers like to put it, the future is "epistemically open" to us, even though it might be causally closed. It is objectively the case that the evolving state of the cosmos produces new and surprising configurations of matter and energy, including the very thoughts that arise as you read these words. The fact that all this flows from prior conditions by routes determined by physical, biological, and other natural laws, some yet to be discovered, subtracts nothing from its newness. And the fact that human desires drive outcomes (along with other factors) means that change is often to our benefit: we can and do make progress in many domains of human striving, even if the process is deterministic. And again, should any indeterminism or randomness play a role in behavior, it likely wouldn't add to our ability to make progress.

Rationality

Some suppose that the only way we can be rational creatures, capable of knowing truths about the world and acting effectively in light of these truths, is by being causally disconnected from nature in some respect. They believe there's a conflict between being fully caused and being rational. But if we were causally disconnected from the world in some way, having our perceptions, our consideration of evidence, our thoughts, and practical conclusions without being *determined* in having them, how would this make us more rational, or help us better understand reality? Some animals, as a result of natural selection and presumably without contra-causal free will, got to be better and better predictors of what they would encounter in the world.

Those that made the evolutionary cut did so by constructing more reliable and accurate models of reality than did their competitors. As rather sophisticated, all too competitive cognitive systems, we're now *very* good at modeling our environment, and any causal disconnection between the environment and the model would degrade, not improve, the model's accuracy. Any part of us outside the causal network, anything radically free to choose its response or evaluation, would necessarily be *uninfluenced* by the world, *unresponsive* to it, and so couldn't *know* anything about it. Stepping outside of macro-level determinism, unlikely in any case, wouldn't give us a better handle on reality. So there's no conflict between being determined to have a view of things and having a true, accurate view. It's just that some deterministic systems (scientists, for instance) do a better job of modeling the world than others (astrologers and palm readers) by virtue of *how* they model it.

Meaning

The Big Question of meaning looms large if we take naturalism seriously, as examined in Chapter 7. Without a supernatural intelligence to define a purpose for the universe, there isn't any intrinsic point to existence, considered as a whole. We are, ultimately, just here, doing what we do. We exist not because anyone or anything thought it was necessary, but only because we happen to have arisen by virtue of natural causes. So regrettably (some think), we must put aside dreams of a final purpose and content ourselves with local meanings derived from our contingent human nature. But must we necessarily regret this lack of ultimate meaning?

That many do regret it on occasion is undeniable. We are hard-wired to seek agency and purpose in events, and when we discover that the universe is inscrutable, existentially speaking, that can be unsettling. But we are not entitled to remain upset for long, since it turns out that such meaning simply isn't possible. Were we to discover that our world was created with someone's purpose in mind, we would simply ask the next obvious question: why does *that* entity exist? Where did *it* come from? What's the point of *its* purposes? Our ability to ask such questions undermines the very basis for ultimate meaning. Therefore, we can't shake our fist at the universe for its inscrutability, nor can we legitimately characterize it as *intrinsically* meaningless, since that's to project upon it our assumption that it should be meaningful. Existence, in itself, necessarily transcends the meaningful/meaningless distinction – it simply *is*.

So while it's true that naturalism discovers no ultimate purpose in things, that's only a problem because of our psychology, not the world. And besides, there's a good deal of existential joy to be found in relishing the fact that we are *not* relegated to playing a role in someone else's cosmic drama, that we are part of a process that unfolds on its own, quite unexpectedly and for no obvious reason. It's possible to feel that this is a *better* existential situation than being confined to a purpose, which is good, since that's how things really are. And besides, the local purposes generated by our human-scale projects survive quite handily under naturalism (as they do under most worldviews), and such purposes give life plenty of meaning.

Reductionism

People sometimes confuse naturalism with what philosopher Daniel Dennett has called "greedy" reductionism, the idea that complex, higher-order phenomena (persons, minds, beliefs, money, government) can be understood or explained at the physical level of their most basic constituent parts, such as atoms and molecules. Of course this can't be done, since many higher-order phenomena exhibit properties that can only be understood as outcomes of processes involving entities and processes *well above* the level of atoms and molecules – things such as proteins, cells, neural structures and perceptual systems. Understanding phenomena this way involves a *benign* reductionism that's the hallmark of a good deal of science: nothing but the entities and processes at lower and intermediate levels, properly organized, is needed to explain the emergence of new, higher-order phenomena. Nothing spooky or mysterious is involved; rather, we get "something more from nothing but," as biologist Ursula Goodenough puts it.

It's sometimes supposed that even this sort of benign reductionism, if successful, *eliminates* higher-order phenomena as existing in their own right. But this doesn't follow. Explaining complex things in terms of the organization and interaction of simpler parts and processes doesn't make them disappear. They are just as real as their constituent parts.

Of course, few take the possibility of eliminative reductionism very seriously, except as a straw man with which to incite fear of deterministic causal explanations. An example is the claim that if we are composed only of physical, chemical and biological processes that obey various natural causal laws, the person-level causality of our reasons and motives is somehow invalidated or made irrelevant. But of course this is false. Individuals and their causal powers don't disappear just because their parts are physical and behave deterministically. We can't usefully explain our behavior to ourselves without invoking persons and their reasons and motives. That's what justifies the scientific, empirical claim that people are *real*, just as real as atoms and molecules (not that you needed science to reassure you on that point). Nevertheless, it's important to remember that this doesn't mean that people and their actions aren't fully caused. Even though our behavior *qua* behavior can't be usefully explained at the basic physical or chemical level, we have every reason to suppose it's still amenable to causal explanation at higher levels.

Scientism

Naturalism should also not be confused with scientism, the idea that science can or should determine beliefs, attitudes, and behaviors in all domains of human life. To hold a naturalistic worldview is simply to use science to decide about the ultimate constituents of the cosmos and understand how they combine to produce stars, planets, life and human beings; it isn't to suppose that science is the measure of all things. Like everyone else, naturalists don't apply science and causal analysis to every aspect of human existence, nor do we think this is either wise or feasible. Understanding how things work is just one part of life. Love, art, music, aesthetics, history, drama, literature, dance, cuisine, and dozens of other aspects of life and learning involve appreciations and techniques that have little or nothing to do with the scientific project, even though everything that goes on in such endeavors is composed of the ultimate constituents of the cosmos, according to science. Scientism is a bit like the greedy reductionism that people properly reject (see above), but that scientists are seldom guilty of, and that naturalists should avoid as well. This isn't difficult since a great deal of human experience arises in contexts that are naturally non-cognitive, or that involve goals, skills and techniques having nothing to do with explaining the world or how things work.

Appendix B

Quotes on Free Will

Some of our best known philosophical and political forbearers, including Thomas Jefferson and Abraham Lincoln, were skeptical about contra-causal free will. These well-respected, well-informed and rather famous people doubted the idea that human beings are causally privileged over the natural world, in which case maybe we should doubt it too. This of course doesn't count as a scientific or philosophical argument, but it might give believers in contra-causal free will some pause. And just because those quoted below are smart individuals who challenge conventional wisdom in remarkably similar ways, given their geographical and temporal diversity, doesn't mean they're wrong. You, as did they, should make up your mind about free will on the merits, carefully considering your actual experience of choice (as did David Hume), the evidence from science (as did Einstein and Darwin), and the impossibility of being a self-caused self (as did Nietzsche and many other philosophers). If you're already in agreement with what the French *philosophes*, Jefferson, Lincoln, Darwin, Einstein and Mark Twain said about free will, just enjoy the ride, which is more or less in alphabetical, not chronological, order.

Clarence Darrow, celebrated defense attorney, lawyer for John Scopes in the 1925 "Monkey Trial": "Every one knows that the heavenly bodies move in certain paths in relation to each other with seeming consistency and regularity which we call [physical] law... No one attributes freewill or motive to the material world. Is the conduct of man or the other animals any more subject to whim or choice than the action of the planets?... We know that man's every act is induced by motives that led or urged him here or there; that the sequence of cause and effect runs through the whole universe, and is nowhere more compelling than with man." Quoted by Norman Swartz at http://www.sfu.ca/philosophy/swartz/freewill1.htm.

Charles Darwin: "...one doubts existence of free will [because] every action [is] determined by heredity, constitution, example of others or teaching of others."

And: "This view should teach one profound humility, one deserves no credit for anything...nor ought one to blame others." From Darwin's notebooks, quoted by Robert Wright in *The Moral Animal*, pp. 349-50.

Baron D'Holbach: "The inward persuasion that we are free to do, or not to do a thing, is but a mere illusion. If we trace the true principle of our actions, we shall find, that they are always necessary consequences of our volitions and desires, which are never in our power. You think yourself free, because you do what you will; but are you free to will, or not to will; to desire, or not to desire? Are not your volitions and desires necessarily excited by objects or qualities totally independent of you?" From *Good Sense Without God*.

Albert Einstein: "If the moon, in the act of completing its eternal way around the earth, were gifted with self-consciousness, it would feel thoroughly convinced that it was traveling its way of its own accord on the strength of a resolution taken once and for all. So would a Being, endowed with higher insight and more perfect intelligence, watching man and his doings, smile about man's illusion that he was acting according to his own free will." From a piece written as homage to the Indian mystical poet Rabindranath Tagore.

And: "I do not believe in free will. Schopenhauer's words, 'Man can do what he wants, but he cannot will what he wills,' accompany me in all situations throughout my life and reconcile me with the actions of others, even if they are rather painful to me. This awareness of the lack of free will keeps me from taking myself and my fellow men too seriously as acting and deciding individuals, and from losing my temper." From "My Credo."

Thomas Jefferson: "I should . . . prefer swallowing one incomprehensibility rather than two. It requires one effort only to admit the single incomprehensibility of matter endowed with thought, and two to believe, first that of an existence called spirit, of which we have neither evidence nor idea, and then secondly how that spirit, which has neither extension nor solidity, can put material organs into motion." From a letter to John Adams, March, 1820.

Abraham Lincoln: "The human mind is impelled to action, or held in rest by some power, over which the mind itself has no control." From "Handbill Replying to Charges of Infidelity."

And: "[Lincoln and I] often argued the question, I taking the opposite view... I once contended that man was free and could act without a motive. He smiled at my philosophy, and answered that it was impossible, because the motive was born before the man... He defied me to act without motive and unselfishly; and when I did the act and told him of it, he analyzed and sifted it to the last grain. After he had concluded, I could not avoid the admission that he had demonstrated the absolute selfishness of the entire act." From William H. Herndon, "Analysis of the Character of Abraham Lincoln," *Abraham Lincoln Quarterly* 1 (Dec. 1941): 411, quoted in "Abraham Lincoln and the Doctrine of Necessity" by Allen C. Guezlo.

Friedrich Nietzsche: "The *causa sui* [self-caused self] is the best self-contradiction that has been conceived so far; it is a sort of rape and perversion of logic. But the extravagant pride of man has managed to entangle itself profoundly and frightfully with just this nonsense. The desire for 'freedom of the will' in the superlative metaphysical sense, which still holds sway, unfortunately, in the minds of the half-educated; the desire to bear the entire and ultimate responsibility for one's actions oneself, and to absolve God, the world, ancestors, chance, and society involves nothing less than to be precisely this *causa sui* and, with more than Baron Münchhausen's audacity, to pull oneself up into existence by the hair, out of the swamps of nothingness." From *Beyond Good and Evil*.

Bertrand Russell: "When a man acts in ways that annoy us we wish to think him wicked, and we refuse to face the fact that his annoying behavior is the result of antecedent causes which, if you follow them long enough, will take you beyond the moment of his birth, and therefore to events for which he cannot be held responsible by any stretch of imagination… When a motorcar fails to start, we do not attribute its annoying behavior to sin, we do not say, you are a wicked motorcar, and you shall not have any more gasoline until you go." From "Has Religion Made Useful Contributions to Civilization?" at http://www.update.uu.se/~fbendz/library/has_reli.htm#freewill.

Arthur Schopenhauer: "You are free to do what you want, but you are not free to want what you want."

Baruch Spinoza: "The mind is determined to this or that choice by a cause which is also determined by another cause, and this again by another, and so on *ad infinitum*. This doctrine teaches us to hate no one, to despise no one, to mock no one, to be angry with no one, and to envy no one."

Mark Twain: "Where are there are two desires in a man's heart he has no choice between the two but must obey the strongest, there being no such thing as free will in the composition of any human being that ever lived." From *Mark Twain in Eruption*, Bernard Devoto, editor. See also and especially "What Is Man?" for Twain's completely naturalistic view on human nature, at http://users.telerama.com/~joseph/wman.html.

Voltaire: "Now, you receive all your ideas; therefore you receive your wish, you wish therefore necessarily. The word 'liberty' does not therefore belong in any way to your will... The will, therefore, is not a faculty that one can call free. A free will is an expression absolutely void of sense, and what the scholastics have called will of indifference, that is to say willing without cause, is a chimera unworthy of being combated." From Voltaire's "Philosophical Dictionary."

Appendix C
Resources and Readings

Web Sites

Organizations

Center for Naturalism: *www.centerfornaturalism.org*

Secular Coalition of America: *www.secular.org*

Secular Web: *www.infidels.org*

American Humanist Association: *www.americanhumanist.org*

Council for Secular Humanism: *www.secularhumanism.org*

Skeptic Society: *www.skeptic.com*

United for a Fair Economy: *www.faireconomy.org*

On Naturalism

Naturalism.Org: *www.naturalism.org*

Richard Carrier's book and articles on naturalism: *www.columbia.edu/~rcc20/naturalism.html*

Internet Encyclopedia of Philosophy: *www.iep.utm.edu/n/naturali.htm*

Wikipedia on metaphysical naturalism as a worldview: *http://en.wikipedia.org/wiki/Metaphysical_naturalism*

Wikipedia on philosophical naturalism: *http://en.wikipedia. org/wiki/Naturalism_%28philosophy%29*

Stanford Encyclopedia of Philosophy on naturalism: *http://plato.stanford.edu/entries/naturalism*

Stanford Encyclopedia of Philosophy on naturalism and ethics: *http://plato.stanford.edu/entries/naturalism-moral*

Secular Web pages on naturalism: *www.infidels.org/library/ modern/nontheism/naturalism*

Ted Honderich's website on determinism and freedom: *www.ucl. ac.uk/~uctytho/dfwIntroIndex.htm*

Books

Julian Baggini: *Atheism: A Very Short Introduction*

James K. Beilby, editor: *Naturalism Defeated?: Essays on Plantinga's Evolutionary Argument Against Naturalism*

Susan Blackmore: *The Meme Machine*; *Conversations on Consciousness*

Paul Bloom: *Descartes Baby: How the Science of Child Development Explains What Makes Us Human*

Paul Breer: *The Spontaneous Self: Viable Alternatives to Free Will*

Richard Carrier: *Sense and Goodness Without God: A Defense of Metaphysical Naturalism*

William Casebeer: *Natural Ethical Facts*

Patricia Churchland: *Brain-Wise: Studies in Neurophilosophy*

Richard Dawkins: *The Selfish Gene; The Blind Watchmaker; Unweaving the Rainbow; The God Delusion*

Mario De Caro & David Macarthur, editors: *Naturalism In Question*

Daniel Dennett: *Elbow Room; Darwin's Dangerous Idea; Freedom Evolves; Breaking the Spell*

Jared Diamond: *Collapse: How Societies Choose to Fail or Succeed*

Richard Double: *The Non-Reality of Free Will*

Gary Drescher: *Good and Real: Demystifying Paradoxes from Physics to Ethics*

Owen Flanagan: *The Problem of the Soul*

Ursula Goodenough: *The Sacred Depths of Nature*

Sam Harris: *The End of Faith; Letter to a Christian Nation*

James F. Haught: *Is Nature Enough?: Meaning and Truth in the Age of Science*

Nicholas Humphrey: *How to Solve the Mind-Body Problem; Seeing Red*

Robert Kane, editor: *The Oxford Handbook of Free Will*

Marc Hauser: *Moral Minds: How Nature Designed Our Universal Sense of Right and Wrong*

Ted Honderich: *How Free Are You?; Punishment: The Supposed Justifications Revisited*

Thomas Metzinger: *Being No One: The Self-Model Theory of Subjectivity*

Chris Mooney: *The Republican War on Science*

William R. Murry: *Reason and Reverence: Religious Humanism for the 21st Century*

Derk Pereboom: *Living Without Free Will*

Steven Pinker: *The Blank Slate*, esp. chapter 10, "Fear of Determinism"

Heidi Ravven (forthcoming): *Searching For Ethics In A New America*

Chet Raymo: *Skeptics and True Believers*

Janet Radcliffe Richards: *Human Nature After Darwin*

Matt Ridley: *The Origins of Virtue: Human Instincts and the Evolution of Cooperation*

Lee Silver: *Challenging Nature: The Clash of Science and Spirituality at the New Frontiers of Life.*

Michael Shermer: *Why People Believe Weird Things: Pseudoscience, Superstition, and Other Confusions of Our Time*

B.F. Skinner: *Beyond Freedom and Dignity*; *About Behaviorism*

Saul Smilansky: *Free Will and Illusion*

Keith Stanovich: *The Robot's Rebellion: Finding Meaning in the Age of Darwin*

Twyla Tharp: *The Creative Habit: Learn It and Use It for Life*

Franz de Waal: *Good Natured: The Origins of Right and Wrong in Humans and Other Animals*

Bruce Waller: *The Natural Selection of Autonomy*; *Freedom Without Responsibility*

Daniel Wegner: *The Illusion of Conscious Will*

Peter Wenz: *Abortion Rights as Religious Freedom*

Edward O. Wilson: *Consilience: The Unity of Knowledge*; *The Future of Life*; *The Creation*

Robert Wright: *The Moral Animal*

About the Center for Naturalism

The Center for Naturalism (CFN) is a Massachusetts 501(c)3 non-profit educational organization devoted to increasing public awareness of naturalism and its implications for social and personal well-being. By means of local activities, publications, educational programs and policy development, the CFN seeks to foster the understanding that human beings and their behavior are fully caused, entirely natural phenomena, and that human flourishing is best achieved in the light of such understanding.

Center for Naturalism
P.O. Box 441705
Somerville, MA 02144
USA
617-480-8846

www.centerfornaturalism.org
info@naturalism.org

About the author

Thomas W. Clark is founder and director of the Center for Naturalism and creator of Naturalism.Org, among the Web's most comprehensive resources on scientific naturalism and its implications. He lectures and writes on science, naturalism, ethics, free will, criminal justice, consciousness, addiction, and related philosophical and social concerns.

Typesetting and design by Bruce Jones Design, Inc., Norwood, MA
http://www.brucejonesdesign.com

Printing and binding by Acme Bookbinding, Charlestown, MA
http://www.acmebook.com

Front cover: Palatino
Text and back cover: Janson